BIBLE STU

THE Herschel HOBBS COMMENTARY®

by

Robert J. Dean

Fall 2007

Volume 2, Number 1

Send questions/comments to
--Editor, *The Herschel Hobbs Commentary*
--One LifeWay Plaza
--Nashville, TN 37234-0175
--Or make comments on the web at
www.lifeway.com

ACKNOWLEDGMENTS.–We believe the Bible has God for its author; salvation for its end; and truth, without any mixture of error, for its matter and that all Scripture is totally true and trustworthy. The 2000 statement of *The Baptist Faith and Message* is our doctrinal guideline.

The Herschel Hobbs Commentary (ISSN 1550-719X), Bible Studies for Life, is published quarterly by LifeWay Christian Resources of the Southern Baptist Convention, One LifeWay Plaza, Nashville, Tennessee 37234; Thom S. Rainer, President, LifeWay Christian Resources of the Southern Baptist Convention; © Copyright 2007 LifeWay Christian Resources of the Southern Baptist Convention. All rights reserved. Single subscription to individual address, $22.35 per year. If you need help with an order, WRITE LifeWay Church Resources Customer Service, One LifeWay Plaza, Nashville, Tennessee 37234-0113; For subscriptions or subscription changes, FAX (615) 251-5818 or E-MAIL subscribe @lifeway.com. For bulk shipments mailed quarterly to one address, FAX (615) 251-5933, E-MAIL orderentry@lifeway.com., or write to the above address. Please allow six to eight weeks for arrival of first issue.

Printed in the United States of America.

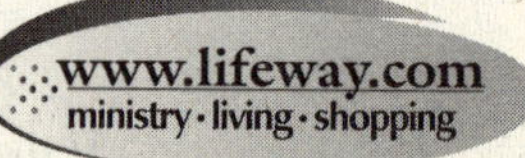

Dedicated to the memory of

Nathan Johnson.

His prayer was to impact his school for Christ.

He shared Christ wherever he was.

Although he died at 16,

his life and witness brought many to Christ.

Contents

Study Theme

Contents

Study Theme

Living for Another World in This World

As Christians, our true citizenship is in heaven (Phil. 3:20). Thus our earthly days should be lived by heaven's standards (Heb. 11:13). These themes are found in many books of the Bible. For example, the first half of the Book of Daniel tells of some young Hebrews who were exiles from their homeland but who strove to be true to the values of the Lord.

The first lesson, "Meeting Cultural Challenges," is based on verses from chapter 1. This is the story of the decision of Daniel and his friends not to defile themselves by eating the king's food. The second lesson, "Feeling Anxious About the Future," is based on verses from Daniel 2. In a dream Nebuchadnezzar saw the kingdom of God shattering all world kingdoms. The third lesson, "Facing the Fiery Furnace," is based on verses from Daniel 3. Shadrach, Meshach, and Abednego refused to bow down before Nebuchadnezzar's image. The fourth lesson, "Handling Success Successfully," is based on verses from Daniel 4. The proud Nebuchadnezzar became insane and lived like an animal until he turned to God. The fifth lesson, "Reading the Handwriting on the Wall," is based on verses from Daniel 5. King Belshazzar saw the handwriting on the wall, and Daniel interpreted its meaning.

The Study Theme Life Impact is designed to help you live for another world in this one by . . .

- exploring the dividing line between capitulating to the expectations and values of the dominant culture and resisting cultural assimilation and then determining to draw the line between worldly cultural assimilation and godly involvement in society (Sept. 2)
- evaluating whether you are anxious about the future, and then deciding to rest in the assurance that God is in control of human history and events and of your life as well (Sept. 9)
- analyzing what it takes to stand for God and refuse to compromise your faith even in the face of grave danger and then assessing what it would take for you to do so (Sept. 16)
- appraising how proud you are and then determining what it would take for you to become humble before the Lord (Sept. 23)
- analyzing how secularized you have become and whether you are glorifying God with your life and then deciding how your life could better honor and glorify God (Sept. 30)

Week of September 2

MEETING CULTURAL CHALLENGES

Background Passage: Daniel 1:1-21
Focal Passage: Daniel 1:3-5,8-15,17-21

❖ *Significance of the Lesson*

• The *Life Question* is, How far am I willing to go in conforming to my culture?

• The *Biblical Truth* is that God's people can be involved in and helpful to their society, but they must draw the line when it comes to allowing themselves to be dominated by their culture.

• The *Life Impact* is designed to help you live for another world in this world by exploring the dividing line between capitulating to the expectations and values of the dominant culture and resisting cultural assimilation and then determining to draw the line between worldly cultural assimilation and godly involvement in society.

Christians and Culture

Culture refers to the set of values, conventions, and social practices of a group. The group expects its members to conform. Normally, this occurs naturally as one is raised in a certain culture. A tension occurs when a person moves from one group to another. Sometimes a number of people raised in a certain group react against the cultural standards. This is sometimes called a "counter culture." The dominant culture is the one held by most people. Some have called Christianity a counter culture because it differs from the dominant secular and religious views of a non-Christian world. Christians cannot conform to their culture's values and practices (Rom. 12:1-2). They must be true to a higher standard, one based on the Bible. One of the strong themes of the Book of Daniel is the way Daniel responded to the culture of pagan Babylon after being raised in the culture of Judah.

The Historical Setting of Daniel

The land of the Jews was on one of the major trade routes between the two earliest centers of power in the ancient world. The early history of Israel was dominated by Egypt. Its later history was influenced by a succession of mighty empires from the east: Assyria, Babylonia, and Persia. Assyria defeated the Northern Kingdom of Israel and threatened the Southern Kingdom. But in 605 B.C. the Babylonian army of King Nebuchadnezzar defeated the Assyrians at the battle of Carchemish. Shortly after this the Babylonians extended their influence into Judah. Jehoiakim, the king of Judah, had been subject to Assyria, so he soon rebelled against Babylonia. Nebuchadnezzar easily defeated Judah. The Book of Daniel emphasizes the sovereignty of God. The reason for these events was that "the Lord gave Jehoiakim king of Judah into his hand" (Dan. 1:2). As a way of showing dominance over Judah, Nebuchadnezzar carried from the temple many valuable vessels and placed them in the temple of his god. At the same time he took from Judah its finest young men to be trained for service in Shinar, another name for Babylon. This was the first of three phases of the Jewish exile. The final one came in 586 B.C. when Nebuchadnezzar destroyed the temple and carried many people to Babylon.

❖ *Search the Scriptures*

Daniel and his three friends were among a group of young men brought to Babylon by Nebuchadnezzar in 605 B.C. They were to be trained for three years with the aim of bringing them into service for Nebuchadnezzar. For this the young men needed to be trained in Babylonian culture, language, and customs. As part of their training, they were to be wined and dined with royal culinary delights. Daniel went along with the training, but he determined not to eat the king's meat or drink his wine. He asked the official to allow him 10 days to show that he and his friends would be fit and healthy on their own diet. At some risk, the official allowed the test. At the end of the test period, the four young men were healthier than those who ate the king's fare. God gave great success in their learning to Daniel and his three friends. Even the king was impressed. They began to serve the king, something Daniel did for 40 years, and he served the Persians who defeated the Babylonians.

Expectation of Cultural Assimilation (Dan. 1:3-5)

Who was Ashpenaz? At what age were the children chosen? What were their qualifications? What were they expected to learn? What was expected to be their diet? What were they being prepared to do? How are we affected by an expectation of cultural assimilation?

Verses 3-5: **And the king spake unto Ashpenaz the master of his eunuchs, that he should bring certain of the children of Israel, and of the king's seed, and of the princes; [4]children in whom was no blemish, but well-favored, and skilful in all wisdom, and cunning in knowledge, and understanding science, and such as had ability in them to stand in the king's palace, and whom they might teach the learning and the tongue of the Chaldeans. [5]And the king appointed them a daily provision of the king's meat, and of the wine which he drank: so nourishing them three years, that at the end thereof they might stand before the king.**

The word *assimilation* refers to the process of being made similar to something, in this case to assimilate or be absorbed into the culture of a population or dominant group. The Babylonians knew that the young Jews had been trained in the ways of their own people. To be useful to Babylonia, they needed to unlearn some past learning and replace it with new understandings.

The task of training the young Jews was given to **Ashpenaz** [ASH-peh-naz], **the master of** the **eunuchs.** The word translated **eunuchs** at times referred to literal eunuchs (Isa. 56:3), but it also could refer to an official in the government ("court officials," HCSB). For example, this word was used in Genesis 37:36 to describe Potiphar, and he was married. Thus Ashpenaz need not have been a eunuch; nor does his title as **the master of** the **eunuchs** necessarily imply that Daniel and the other Jews were eunuchs. Ashpenaz had an important task—to prepare these Jews to serve in the Babylonian government.

The word translated **children** does not refer to small children. The Hebrew word could refer to children, boys, and young men below the age of 20. Daniel was probably about 17 and his friends a few years younger, at about 14. Thus they were old enough to be trained and young enough to be assimilated into a different culture.

These young men had qualifications other than age. They were **of the king's seed, and of the princes** ("from the royal family and from the nobility," HCSB). This shows that Nebuchadnezzar was robbing Judah of its source for future leaders.

They were to have **no blemish** ("without any physical defect," HCSB). This rules out eunuchs and other physically handicapped people. They also had to be **well-favored** ("good looking," HCSB). Their health and good appearance would enhance their usefulness in government service.

Intelligence was absolutely essential in selecting the ones to be trained. Several words and phrases in verse 4 describe various aspects of their intelligence. **Skilful in all wisdom** means "showing aptitude for every kind of learning" (NIV). It refers to having insight and comprehension. **Cunning in knowledge** refers to the ability to acquire knowledge because they were intelligent. **Understanding science** means that they were "perceptive" (HCSB) or "quick to understand" (NIV). At the end of their training, the candidates needed to be capable **to stand in the king's palace** ("capable of serving in the king's palace," HCSB).

Their curriculum was **the learning and the tongue of the Chaldeans** ("the Chaldean language and literature," HCSB). *Chaldea* was another name for Babylonia. The Assyrians had accumulated a huge library of clay tablets on all subjects. The young Jews had access to this library that the Babylonians had preserved and enlarged.

If they were to serve the king, these young Jews also needed to learn to enjoy the kind of food and drink that the king ate and drank. Therefore, "the king assigned them daily provisions from the royal food and from the wine that he drank" (HCSB). The king probably viewed this as one of the rewards of their training. He expected this to contribute to their becoming fit after three years of training "to serve in the king's court" (HCSB).

The king probably anticipated total obedience to the expectations of verses 3-5. From his point of view, he had given great privileges to these young men. As captives, they could have been treated much worse.

Verses 6-7 give a further clue to the king's objective in dealing with the Jews. He changed their names from Jewish to Babylonian names. The Bible focuses on Daniel and his three friends. Their Jewish names all contained some part of the name of their God. Their new names all contained some part of the name of one of the gods of the Babylonians. Daniel ("God judges") became Belteshazzar [bel-tih-SHAZ-uhr] ("Bel [or Marduk] protect the king's life"). Hananiah [han-uh-NIGH-uh] ("the LORD has been gracious") became Shadrach [SHAD-rak] ("command of Aku" [the Sumerian moon god]). Mishael [MISH-eh-uhl] ("who is what God is") became Meshach [MEE-shak] ("who is what

Aku is"). Azariah [az-uh-RIGH-uh] ("the LORD has helped") became Abed-nego [uh-BED-nih-goh] ("servant of Nebo" [or Nabu]). By changing the young men's names the Babylonians were signifying that their gods were stronger than the Hebrew God.

Verses 3-7 describe the cultural expectations of the young Jews brought to Babylon to be trained for government service. The culture demanded obedience to its expectations, which would result in assimilation into the culture. What does your culture expect of you? A crisis point is a change from one culture to another. Many children of Christian parents are comfortable during childhood with the cultural expectations of their parents. Then as they become independent, they are confronted by the expectations of a different culture. It may be a secular youth culture, a military culture, a college culture, a company's corporate culture, or just the expectations of a secular culture that at best gives only lip service to Christian faith and biblical values. How do people respond to these expectations?

What are the lasting truths in Daniel 1:3-5?

1. Each culture has its own set of expectations.
2. Each culture expects compliance with its values and practices.

Drawing the Line (Dan. 1:8-15)

Where did Daniel draw the line? Why did he do this? How risky was this action? Did he accept all the other cultural expectations? What are different ways of responding to cultural expectations? What test did Daniel propose? What were the results of the test?

Verse 8: **But Daniel purposed in his heart that he would not defile himself with the portion of the king's meat, nor with the wine which he drank: therefore he requested of the prince of the eunuchs that he might not defile himself.**

Daniel was willing to go along with some of the cultural expectations, but he **purposed** ("determined," HCSB; "resolved," NIV) **in his heart that he would not defile himself with the portion of the king's meat, nor with the wine which he drank.** How would these things **defile** him? Two possibilities have been explored. One is that the food of a pagan king would include food that from a Jewish perspective was ceremonially unclean. The other explanation for Daniel's refusal was that the food and drink from the king's table had first been offered to the false gods of the Babylonians. Thus to partake of it would be tantamount to worshiping those gods. Daniel may have been uncomfortable with some of the other expectations, but he chose to make his stand on this point. He had strong convictions against worshiping other gods.

We must not slight how dangerous Daniel's decision was. Stephen R. Miller listed six ways for that it was risky. "(1) To refuse the royal diet could have been taken as an insult to the king and as an act of direct disobedience to Nebuchadnezzar's orders. (2) Pressure from Daniel's peers most certainly made the decision difficult. Everyone else was doing it. By choosing this course of action, Daniel and his friends were setting themselves apart from the others. Now they were different, strange. (3) Such unorthodox behavior could have jeopardized their chances for advancement. (4) The quality of food would have been attractive. It was the best in the land. (5) Their new location may have tempted them to be unfaithful. Judah was nine hundred miles away; parents and friends would never know whether or not they kept God's laws. Yet Daniel and his friends were aware of a very important fact. Other people might not know their actions, but God would know, and someday all will give an account of themselves to him. (6) It would have been natural to argue that since God had not protected them from captivity—this horrible situation—they did not have to be careful to obey his commands. They could have become bitter toward God during this time."[1]

Verses 9-15: **Now God had brought Daniel into favor and tender love with the prince of the eunuchs. [10]And the prince of the eunuchs said unto Daniel, I fear my lord the king, who hath appointed your meat and your drink: for why should he see your faces worse liking than the children which are of your sort? then shall ye make me endanger my head to the king. [11]Then said Daniel to Melzar, whom the prince of the eunuchs had set over Daniel, Hananiah, Mishael, and Azariah, [12]Prove thy servants, I beseech thee, ten days; and let them give us pulse to eat, and water to drink. [13]Then let our countenances be looked upon before thee, and the countenance of the children that eat of the portion of the king's meat: and as thou seest, deal with thy servants. [14]So he consented to them in this matter, and proved them ten days. [15]And at the end of ten days their countenances appeared fairer and fatter in flesh than all the children which did eat the portion of the king's meat.**

When Daniel told the official over them about his plan, the official was frightened. He feared that by refusing the king's food and drink, Daniel would not be as healthy as those who obeyed the king's command. If that happened, he said, "The king would then have my head because of you" (NIV). Daniel knew that his decision was dangerous. If the king learned about it, he would be in trouble. But Daniel had a plan that he hoped would keep it from the king. He proposed a test. He and his three friends would eat vegetables and drink water for **ten days.** Then they would be examined to see how their appearance compared with the other Jewish youths. **Pulse** ("vegetables," NIV, HCSB) translates a Hebrew word "which means basically 'that which grows from sown seed.' The term would include not only vegetables but fruits, grains, and bread that is made from grains. Daniel's diet was similar to many so-called health food diets today. By this request Daniel was not suggesting that eating meat was wrong (see 10:2), for a meat diet was permitted and in some instances even commanded in the law (such as, in the case of the Passover lamb and other sacrifices)."[2]

The Babylonian official agreed to the test because the Lord had given Daniel special favor with him. **Melzar** [MEL-zahr] may be a proper name or the word could be translated "guard" (NIV, HCSB). At the end of the 10 days, Daniel and his friends passed the test; so they were allowed to continue their own special diet.

Daniel's action illustrates the biblical teaching that every believer must draw the line and take a stand when a moral conviction or a biblical truth is at stake. We must not be conformed to a dominant society that expects believers to conform in every way (Rom. 12:1-2). Not every believer would draw the line at the same point, but every Christian should have a line.

A similar issue came up in the Corinthian church. Some drew the line at eating any meat that been offered to idols. Paul did not think this was wrong within itself. He felt it became wrong when it caused a fellow Christian to stumble. "Therefore, if food causes my brother to fall, I will never again eat meat" (1 Cor. 8:13, HCSB). Paul was willing to make some accommodations for the dominant culture in order to win the lost: "I have become all things to all people, so that I may by all means save some" (9:22, HCSB). But Paul drew the line on eating meat in a pagan feast in an idol temple, writing, "You cannot share in the Lord's table and the table of demons" (10:21, HCSB).

There were a variety of attitudes toward the exile. One was total resistance. The people in that group were killed. Others totally compromised and complied with all cultural expectations. Still others were like Daniel. He was not happy with all the cultural expectations, but he went along with many of them. He studied his captors' language and literature. He accepted a position in the Babylonian government. He was uncomfortable with some expectations, but he staked his life on only one issue. Personally, I think he was uncomfortable with the name change. My basis for this is that he never used his Babylonian name when speaking of himself; only the Babylonians used it (Dan. 1:7; 2:26; 4:19; 5:12). However, Daniel did not make a big issue of this as he did with the food. Instead, he adopted a policy of passive noncompliance. He ignored the name change although he did not go to war every time someone called him Belteshazzar.

What are the lasting truths in Daniel 1:8-15?

1. Believers should beware of cultural expectations that are contrary to moral convictions and biblical teachings.
2. Believers must develop the courage and insight of when and how to say no—and then say it.
3. Believers need to have a line beyond which they will not go, but they also need to recognize that not everyone draws the line at the same place.
4. When they reject aspects of pressures to conform to cultural expectations, believers often can do it privately and without fanfare. They simply make a personal commitment and live by God's standards no matter what others are doing.
5. Living according to God's will should have measurable and objective results.

Rendering Service to Society (Dan. 1:17-21)

What was the source of the knowledge and wisdom of Daniel and his friends? Do you think the king was ever told about their special diet? How did the king evaluate the young Jews? How did these young men compare to the king's other advisors? For how long did Daniel serve? What was Daniel's attitude toward service to a pagan king?

Verses 17-21: **As for these four children, God gave them knowledge and skill in all learning and wisdom: and Daniel had understanding in all visions and dreams. [18]Now at the end of the days that the king had said he should bring them in, then the prince of the eunuchs brought them in before Nebuchadnezzar. [19]And the king communed with them; and among them all was found none like Daniel, Hananiah, Mishael, and Azariah: therefore stood they before the king. [20]And in all matters of wisdom and understanding, that the king inquired of them, he found them ten times better than all the magicians and astrologers that were in all his realm. [21]And Daniel continued even unto the first year of king Cyrus.**

After three years, graduation day came. Ashpenaz presented the young Jews to Nebuchadnezzar. We don't know how many there were and whether they all graduated, but we know four who were there. The Bible makes clear that **God gave them knowledge and skill in all learning and wisdom.** In addition, **Daniel had understanding in all visions and dreams.** He had several opportunities to put these skills to work. He interpreted dreams in chapters 2 and 4, interpreted handwriting on the wall in chapter 5, and had a series of visions in chapters 7–12.

The king communed with them means he "interviewed them" (HCSB). In this way he could judge for himself how well they had done in their studies of literature and language. He could tell by looking how healthy they were. Do you think he ever found out that four of the Jews had not followed the prescribed menu? Personally, I doubt that either Ashpenaz or one of the four Jews ever brought that up. When he interviewed them, he was greatly impressed with **Daniel, Hananiah, Mishael, and Azariah.** Notice that their Jewish names are used in verse 19. This is further evidence that Daniel was successful in his passive noncompliance concerning changed names.

Therefore stood they before the king means "they began to serve in the king's court" (HCSB). This had been the purpose of the three years of training (see v. 4). These four received special praise from the king. **He found them ten times better than all the magicians and astrologers that were in all his realm.** That was high praise indeed. Chapters 2 and 4 show examples of how Daniel personally helped Nebuchadnezzar. He interpreted dreams of the king that no one else could interpret.

Many Jews would have condemned Daniel for serving a pagan king, but he was able to bring God's message to the king more than once. He did the same in chapter 5 for Belshazzar [bel-SHAZ-uhr]. Daniel's service **continued even unto the first year of king Cyrus** of Persia. Daniel 10:1 tells us of a vision from the third year of Cyrus. Daniel was an advisor of kings in two of the world's great empires. He served God faithfully as a young man and he continued faithful to old age.

Would this have been possible if as a youth he had failed to draw the line and refused to go against his convictions? Daniel illustrates the importance of decisions made as a youth. The decisions of youth become habits, character, and destiny.

Daniel also illustrates the importance of interacting with the people of the culture in which you live. When Jesus prayed for His disciples,

He did not ask the Father to take them out of the world. Their ministry and service were needed in a sinful, hurting world. Therefore, Jesus asked that they be *in* but not *of* the world (John 17:14-19).

Daniel was a realist. He did not choose to go to Babylon, but he was there. Since the Lord had allowed him to be brought there, he wanted to be faithful and to serve as God wanted him to do. If he were to do this, he needed be true to His God. To do this required that he draw a line and take a stand against what he considered to be idol worship. However, at the same time, he had to maintain contact with the new culture in which he was living.

Billy Graham wrote: "Occasionally I receive letters from Christians who are in great turmoil over their work. Their bosses have demanded they do something illegal or deceptive, or they have been subjected to sexual harassment, or they have discovered fraud or some other illegal activity. These situations are often complex and difficult, and sometimes the right course of action isn't easy to discern. But no matter the cost, I tell them, do your work with honesty and integrity, and don't compromise God's moral standards. It may be difficult, but it's far better to do right than to do wrong. God is with you, and He will not abandon you."[3]

What are the lasting truths in Daniel 1:17-21?

1. Persons of true faith can render valuable service to their society, even though they do not embrace all of its values and standards.

2. Believers are to recognize that whatever gifts and intelligence they have are gifts from God and are to be used in ways that honor Him.

❖ *Spiritual Transformations*

Daniel was taken to Babylon to be trained to serve in Nebuchadnezzar's government. He and his friends were to be trained in the language and literature of Babylonia. They were given Babylonian names and expected to eat what the king provided. Daniel drew the line at eating this food. He asked and received permission to test his own diet for 10 days. He and his three friends passed the test. When they were interviewed by the king at the end of three years of training, he was especially impressed by these four young Jews.

*What pressures have you felt to be in step with the values and practices of your dominant culture?*____________________

____

What pressures call for compromise of moral convictions and biblical truths? ____

____

How do you respond to such pressures? ______________________

____

Prayer of Commitment: Lord, give me the wisdom to know where to draw the line that separates me and my Christian commitments from the practices and expectations of my culture—and give me the strength to draw that line. Amen.

[1]Stephen R. Miller, "Daniel," in *The New American Commentary,* vol. 18 [Nashville: Broadman & Holman Publishers, 1994), 67.

[2]Miller, "Daniel," NAC, 69.

[3]Billy Graham, *The Journey* [Nashville: W Publishing Group, 2006], 235-236.

Week of September 9

FEELING ANXIOUS ABOUT THE FUTURE

Background Passage: Daniel 2:1-49
Focal Passage: Daniel 2:1-3,27-29a,36-44

❖ *Significance of the Lesson*

• The *Life Question* is, Why should I not be anxious about what will happen in the future?

• The *Biblical Truth* is that God's people do not need to be anxious or troubled about the future for God is sovereign and is in control of the kingdoms of this world.

• The *Life Impact* is designed to help you live for another world in this world by evaluating whether you are anxious about the future and then deciding to rest in the assurance that God is in control of human history and events and of your life as well.

Worrying About the Future

Many people worry about the future. Many worry about their own futures. They worry about their children's futures. Some worry about the future of our country and the world as a whole. People of faith do not need to worry about any of these things because they know the God who holds the future. They know that the empires and kingdoms of this world will all pass away. They have confident hope that the kingdom of God is coming and that it will never end.

Dreams As a Means of Revelation

At times in the Bible God revealed certain things through dreams. "We can distinguish three types of dreams. A simple 'message dream' apparently did not need interpretation. For instance, Joseph, in Matthew 1 and 2, understood the dreams concerning Mary and Herod even though no mention is made of interpretation. A second type, the 'simple symbolic dream,' used symbols, but the symbolism was clear enough that the dreamer and others could understand it. In the Old Testament Joseph had this kind of dream in Genesis 37.

'Complex symbolic dreams,' though, needed the interpretive skill of someone with experience or an unusual ability in interpretation. The dreams of Nebuchadnezzar described in Daniel 2 and 4 are good examples of this kind of dream."[1] Another example was the dreams of Pharaoh in Genesis 41. The situations faced by Joseph and Daniel have many similarities. In each case, a king had disturbing dreams, which none of the wise men could explain. In each case God gave the interpretation through a man of faith. A major difference in the two situations was that Nebuchadnezzar demanded that his advisors tell him his dream as well as its meaning.

❖ *Search the Scriptures*

Early in his reign, King Nebuchadnezzar had a dream about the future that left him troubled and anxious. He demanded that his wise men tell him both the dream and its meaning. The king threatened to kill all of them, including Daniel, if they could not reveal the matter. Daniel interpreted the king's dream. It concerned four parts of a huge statue, successive empires beginning with Nebuchadnezzar—with each empire being weaker than the one before. A rock shattered the image, indicating that the Lord God of heaven will establish an everlasting kingdom.

Anxious About the Future (Dan. 2:1-3,27-29a)

When did this event happen? Why was Nebuchadnezzar troubled? How was his anxiety similar to ours? From what groups did he seek help? Why did he demand that someone tell him the dream? Did he have one dream or several? Who was Arioch? Why did Daniel go to him? Where did Daniel get the dream and its interpretation?

Verses 1-3: **And in the second year of the reign of Nebuchadnezzar, Nebuchadnezzar dreamed dreams, wherewith his spirit was troubled, and his sleep brake from him. [2]Then the king commanded to call the magicians, and the astrologers, and the sorcerers, and the Chaldeans, for to show the king his dreams. So they came and stood before the king. [3]And the king said unto them, I have dreamed a dream, and my spirit was troubled to know the dream.**

Some people claim there is a contradiction between the times indicated in Daniel 2:1 and in 1:5. The period for training the young Jews was three years, and they were taken to Babylon in the third year of

Jehoiakim [jih-HOY-uh-kim] (605 B.C.), king of Judah. Yet Daniel 2:1 says that Nebuchadnezzar had his dream in his second year. One explanation would be that the three years were not up and Daniel was still in training. The problem with that is that chapter 1 seems to indicate that Daniel had finished training. Supporting this is also the fact that Nebuchadnezzar considered Daniel one of his advisors (2:13). A better explanation for the seeming difficulty is that the Babylonians did not count the year of accession as the first year of a king's reign and that they counted any part of a year as a year. Nebuchadnezzar ascended the throne in the fall of 605 B.C. Three years of training would end in 603 B.C. Since 605 was not counted as his first year but his accession year, his first year was 604 and his second year would be 603. So Daniel was one of the king's wise men when the king had his troubling dreams.

Nebuchadnezzar dreamed dreams "probably should be understood to indicate that the king was in a state of dreaming rather than that he dreamed several dreams, for the text only reports one."[2] Regardless of how many dreams he had, **his spirit was troubled. Troubled** comes from a root word that means to strike a blow, as with a hammer. This could describe the pounding of his heart, due to fear and anxiety. As a result of his troubled mind and heart, he could not **sleep.** The same word **troubled** is found in Genesis 41:8 to describe Pharaoh, another ruler kept awake by a dream.

Why would this strong, young king be troubled by a dream? No one is immune to all nightmares. He was a warrior who thus far had been successful in battle, but any battle could result in his defeat, even his death. He could be killed in the supposed safety of his palace. Assassinations were fairly common. We are not told why he was troubled, but his anxiety about the future is a mark of the human race. Most of us have fears and worries as we move toward an uncertain future. "We are, perhaps, uniquely among the earth's creatures, the worrying animal. We worry away our lives, fearing the future, discontent with the present, unable to take in the idea of dying, unable to sit still."[3]

The magicians, and the astrologers, and the sorcerers, and the Chaldeans were the groups of supposed wise men whom the king relied on for advice and understanding. For us, **magicians** are people who perform magic tricks to entertain us. For Nebuchadnezzar, they were scribes who recorded the sacred writings. **The astrologers** were supposed to keep in touch with the spirit world, including the dead. **The sorcerers** dabbled in witchcraft and related subjects. **The Chaldeans** were not the same group as in 1:5 but a category of wise men.

In our world, leaders surround themselves with advisors with experience in such fields as the military, economics, diplomacy, finance, law, and politics. These are expected to be wise counselors just as the different kinds of advisors used in ancient times.

Nebuchadnezzar told his advisors **to show the king his dreams** ("to tell him what he had dreamed," NIV). When the advisors appeared before the king, he said, **my spirit was troubled to know the dream** ("I want to know what it means," NIV). He wanted them to help and advise him.

These advisors had books of symbols that they relied on to interpret dreams. They asked the king to tell them his dream and they would explain it. Nebuchadnezzar demanded that they tell him the dream. The *King James Version* says "the thing is gone from me" (v. 5). Other translations have "my word is final" (HCSB) and "this is what I have firmly decided" (NIV). These are different translations of the same Aramaic word (this part of the Book of Daniel was written in Aramaic). According to one view, the king had forgotten the content of the troubling dream. The other view is that he was testing their contact with the gods. If they couldn't tell him his dream, he threatened to kill them and destroy their houses. As they saw the situation, the king was asking the impossible. They said, "No one on earth can make known what the king requests" (v. 10, HCSB). This made the king so furious that he issued orders for executing all his advisors.

Verses 27-29a: **Daniel answered in the presence of the king, and said, The secret which the king hath demanded cannot the wise men, the astrologers, the magicians, the soothsayers, show unto the king; 28but there is a God in heaven that revealeth secrets, and maketh known to the king Nebuchadnezzar what shall be in the latter days. Thy dream, and the visions of thy head upon thy bed, are these; 29aas for thee, O king, thy thoughts came into thy mind upon thy bed, what should come to pass hereafter.**

Daniel and his friends were among the king's advisors who were on the list to be executed. He went to Arioch [EHR-ih-ahk], the official responsible for carrying out the executions. Daniel asked him for time to seek the answer. He asked his three friends to join him in prayer for an answer to the king's questions. When the answer came, he asked to go to the king with the answer he sought.

Daniel told Nebuchadnezzar that no one living or dead could tell him his dream and its meaning. In saying this, he basically agreed with what the Chaldeans said in verse 10, but he added that God could do what humans could not do. Daniel added, **But there is a God in heaven that revealeth secrets.** In his dream, Nebuchadnezzar had been shown some things concerning **the latter days** ("the last days," HCSB) or **what should come to pass hereafter** ("what will happen in the future," HCSB).

Nebuchadnezzar is seen in this lesson as a person who was troubled about his future. Some people should be troubled. Paul preached to Felix about righteousness, self-control, and judgment to come. Felix trembled but made no commitment to the Savior (Acts 24:25).

What are the lasting truths in Daniel 1:1-3,27-29a?

1. Many people are anxious and troubled about things that may happen in the future.

2. Some people are living sinful lives and should be anxious about the future.

3. God's people do not know the details of the rest of their lives, but they do know God is with them and they can trust Him for the future.

Empires Come and Empires Go (Dan. 2:36-43)

What was the vision Nebuchadnezzar saw in his dream? How did Daniel explain the meaning of the king's dream? How do this vision and its interpretation fit with other Bible passages?

Verses 36-43: **This is the dream; and we will tell the interpretation thereof before the king. 37Thou, O king, art a king of kings: for the God of heaven hath given thee a kingdom, power, and strength, and glory. 38And wheresoever the children of men dwell, the beasts of the field and the fowls of the heaven hath he given into thine hand, and hath made thee ruler over them all. Thou art this head of gold. 39And after thee shall arise another kingdom inferior to thee, and another third kingdom of brass, which shall bear rule over all the earth. 40And the fourth kingdom shall be strong as iron: forasmuch as iron breaketh in pieces and subdueth all things: and as iron that breaketh all these, shall it break in pieces and bruise. 41And whereas thou sawest the feet and toes, part of potters' clay, and part of iron, the kingdom shall be divided; but there shall be in it of the strength of the iron, forasmuch as thou sawest the iron mixed**

with miry clay. [42]And as the toes of the feet were part of iron, and part of clay, so the kingdom shall be partly strong, and partly broken. [43]And whereas thou sawest iron mixed with miry clay, they shall mingle themselves with the seed of men: but they shall not cleave one to another, even as iron is not mixed with clay.

Remember, Nebuchadnezzar had not told the content of his troubling dream but insisted that one of the wise men tell him his dream. Either he had forgotten his dream or he was testing his wise men. Thus he expected Daniel to begin by reminding him what he dreamed. Daniel told Nebuchadnezzar his dream in verses 31-35. He said the king saw a colossal statue. It was huge, dazzling, and terrifying.

Then in verses 36-45 Daniel gave **the interpretation.** Daniel called Nebuchadnezzar **a king of kings,** but lest the king be swelled with pride, the prophet gave the credit for this to God: **The God of heaven hath given thee a kingdom, power, and strength, and glory.** All the king's victories had come from the God of the Jews. In allowing the Babylonian king to conquer the people of Judah, God was working out His will.

Daniel identified the **head of gold** on the statue as Nebuchadnezzar and the Babylonian Empire. God had given him dominion over not only people but also over animals and birds. This was the first of four kingdoms in verses 36-43. There is no debate about identifying this first kingdom, but there are differences of opinion about the identity of the other three kingdoms. After Daniel finished, Nebuchadnezzar was exhilarated by what Daniel had said. Apparently Nebuchadnezzar failed to notice that his kingdom, although superior to the others, had an end. Perhaps he took comfort that the end of Babylonia would not be in his lifetime.

A historical review of ancient history kingdom might help. The Babylonian Empire was not the first world empire. There were earlier ones in Egypt and in Assyria. There was even an earlier kingdom of Babylonia, so historians call Nebuchadnezzar's kingdom the Neo-Babylonian Empire. It began with the defeat of Assyria in 605 B.C. and lasted to 539 B. C. when the Persian Empire assumed dominance. The Persian Empire lasted to 331 B.C. when Alexander the Great conquered the world in the name of Greece. He died young and his kingdom was divided among four of his generals, the two most important for the Jews being the Ptolemy kings of Egypt and the Seleucid kings of Syria. Judea was dominated by first one and then the other. Antiochus Epiphanes of Syria persecuted the Jews and desecrated their temple.

The Maccabean family led a revolt that resulted in a century of Jewish independence (165 B.C.), before the Roman general Pompey brought Palestine under Roman control in 63 B.C. The Roman Empire lasted longer and covered more territory than its predecessors. The Western Roman Empire lasted until A.D. 476 and the Eastern Roman Empire until A.D. 1453.

Daniel 2:37-43 mentions four kingdoms. The first was the neo-Babylonian. It was followed by the Persian, which was **inferior to** the neo-Babylonian. This gave way to the Greek, and the fourth was the Roman. Some Bible students think the Greek Empire was the fourth. They do this be dividing the Medes from the Persians (who had conquered the Babylonian Empire through their coalition) or by dividing Alexander's empire from that of his generals.

Notice several things about the list as a whole. For one thing, each kingdom is represented by less expensive materials: from gold to silver to brass to iron to a mixture of iron and clay. Scholars puzzle about what this means. The metals do not represent size or length, because the kingdoms got larger and lasted longer. One explanation is that there was a moral decline in human history with each kingdom. "Through the portrayal of each subsequent empire as inferior to its predecessor, Daniel seems to have been suggesting that the sinfulness of the world would continue to increase until the culmination of history. . . . According to Daniel, the world's kingdoms are not moving toward utopia but in the opposite direction."[4]

Several things are obvious from this passage. All earthly kingdoms are transient or temporary. Each prospers and comes to an end. There have been many kingdoms and nations that have come and gone since Daniel's day. Often boastful leaders make more of their glory than is justified as they and their kingdoms soon are lost beneath the shifting sands of human history. Shelley well captured this in his poem "Ozymandias."

> I met a traveler from an antique land
> Who said: "Two vast and trunkless legs of stone
> Stand in the desert. Near them, on the sand,
> Half sunk, a shattered visage lies, whose frown,
> And wrinkled lip, and sneer of cold command,
> Tell that the sculptor well those passions read
> Which yet survive, stamped on these lifeless things,
> The hand that mocked them, and the heart that fed.
> And on the pedestal these words appear—

'My name is Ozymandias, king of kings:
Look on My works, ye Mighty, and despair!'
Nothing beside remains. Round the decay
Of that colossal wreck, boundless and bare
The lone and level sands stretch far away."[5]

What are the lasting truths in Daniel 2:36-43?

1. The world's superpowers are not here to stay. One succumbs to another. People of biblical faith need to recognize that even the most stable political entities are temporary and transitory. Thus we need to live accordingly.

2. All sovereignty, power, strength, and glory that rulers and nations have ultimately come from God.

3. God is sovereign over human history. He moves in the affairs of nations to bring in His kingdom.

God's Kingdom Is Forever (Dan. 2:44)

What does the rock signify? In what sense did the kingdom come through the work of Jesus Christ? In what sense is the kingdom yet to come? How does belief in God's kingdom help Christians face the future with courage and hope?

Verse 44: **And in the days of these kings shall the God of heaven set up a kingdom, which shall never be destroyed: and the kingdom shall not be left to other people, but it shall break in pieces and consume all these kingdoms, and it shall stand forever.**

In reminding Nebuchadnezzar of his dream, Daniel said, "As you were watching, a stone broke off without a hand touching it, struck the statue on its feet of iron and fired clay, and crushed them. Then the iron, the fired clay, the bronze, the silver, and the gold were shattered and became like chaff from the summer threshing floors" (v. 34, HCSB). If the fourth kingdom was Rome, when did or will this stone hit it? Or to put the question another way: When does God's kingdom destroy the other kingdoms by striking Rome?

Answers to this question are generally consistent with a person's view of God's kingdom. Some emphasize a spiritual reign of Christ that is rooted in His incarnate work of redemption. Jesus preached that "the kingdom of heaven is at hand" (Matt. 4:17). But He also said to pray, "Thy kingdom come" (6:10), and He and His followers spoke of His second coming as the time of ultimate fulfillment (24:27). Other Bible students point to the Old Testament prophecies of Israel's future kingdom in connection with the millennium and ultimately the new heavens and new earth. Many Christians do not have the future charted out, but they do believe that God in His own will and way will bring to an end all earthly kingdoms and establish His own everlasting kingdom. As the seventh angel announced in Revelation 11:15: "The kingdoms of this world are become the kingdoms of our Lord, and of his Christ; and he shall reign forever and ever." Hebrews 12:26-28 describes a time when God will shake all things. When this happens, all things earthly and transient will fall. All that will withstand the shaking are the eternal things of God's eternal kingdom.

How does your faith in God's ultimate victory over evil help you as you face personal, family, work, and world situations that create fear and anxiety? Often we discover that the things we worry about never happen. Someone has said that we ought not to worry about any aspect of an unknown future if we know the ultimate outcome. But what of those things that we worry about that do happen? Rather than worrying about a possible disease, check it out and do something about it. Of course sometimes our worse fears are realized. At such times believers find strength to endure even unto death.

Still anxiety plagues our lives. A couple was watching the news on television, which brings the world into our homes. No previous generation was so quickly informed of troubles everywhere in the world. The wife asked her husband, "Aren't you glad you don't have the president's worries?" He replied, "What are you talking about? I've got my worries and his worries too!"

In a book called *Prescription for Anxiety*, the author wrote: "This little book will not be the slightest use to a person who never worries and who does not know what it is to be plagued by anxious fears. It may be of help to people who are accused—and 'accused' is the word because they are made to feel guilty—of having 'nerves,' of being worried and frightened, and who are sometimes sleepless and frequently depressed, weary and unhappy, especially in the mornings; who have vague fears, the origin and cause of which they cannot trace."[6] If we are honest, most human beings can identify with something in that list.

We are not told Daniel's feelings in the crises of his life, but we know that he faced the kinds of situations that cause people to be anxious about the future. He was uprooted from his homeland and taken to serve a pagan king in a foreign land. He was expected to conform to the customs of the foreign land. In chapter 2, he was the only one who might stop the frustrated king from killing him and all the royal advisors. He believed that the Lord had put him in that place and in that situation for a purpose and that God would give him what he needed to meet the challenge. Thus he prayed and he asked his friends to pray that the Lord would enable him to do the impossible. Behind these actions was his faith in a sovereign God who promised to be with him and to give him what he needed to do God's will.

Therefore, faith in a sovereign and loving God helps us face situations that could create fears and worries as we move toward an unknown future.

I know not what the future hath
Of marvel or surprise,
Assured alone that life and death
His mercy underlies.

. . . .

I know not where His islands lift
Their fronded palms in air;
I only know I cannot drift
Beyond His love and care.[7]

What are the lasting truths in Daniel 2:44?

1. God's kingdom will come, destroying all earthly kingdoms and establishing God's eternal reign.

2. This assurance gives people of faith what they need to face an unknown future in the kingdoms of this world.

❖ *Spiritual Transformations*

Nebuchadnezzar had a troubling dream. He threatened with death all his advisors if one of them could not tell him his dream and its meaning. Daniel, who was one of his young advisors, told the king that God would give Daniel the answer to the king's demands. After Daniel and his friends prayed, God told Daniel what the king demanded, and Daniel in turn told the king. Daniel interpreted the dream as revelation that earthly kingdoms come and go but God's kingdom is eternal.

*Do you ever worry about what the future holds for you?*__________

*What aspects of an unknown future do you sometimes worry about?*____

*How does your Christian faith provide resources for dealing with fears and anxieties about the future?*____________________________

Prayer of Commitment: Lord, help me face an unknown future with faith in Your power and love. Amen.

[1]Albert F. Bean, "Dreams," in the *Holman Illustrated Bible Dictionary* [Nashville: Holman Reference, 2003], 442.

[2]Miller, "Daniel," NAC, 77.

[3]Lewis Thomas, in *Familiar Quotations,* edited by John Bartlett, 15th edition revised and enlarged [Boston: Little, Brown and Company, 1980], 884.

[4]Miller, "Daniel," NAC, 94.

[5]Percy Bysshe Shelley, "Ozymandias," quoted in *Masterpieces of Religious Verse,* edited by James Dalton Morrison [New York: Harper & Row, Publishers, 1948], 311.

[6]Leslie D. Weatherhead, *Prescription for Anxiety* [Nashville: Abingdon Press, 1956], 7.

[7]John Greenleaf Whittier, "The Eternal Goodness," in *Masterpieces of Religious Verse,* 70.

Week of September 16

FACING THE FIERY FURNACE

Background Passage: Daniel 3:1-30

Focal Passage: Daniel 3:1-2,4-6,8,12-14,16-18,24-26,28

❖ *Significance of the Lesson*

• The *Life Question* is, How far am I willing to go in standing for my faith?

• The *Biblical Truth* is that when believers are called on to stand publicly for their faith, they must refuse to compromise.

• The *Life Impact* is designed to help you live for another world in this world by analyzing what it takes to stand for God and refuse to compromise your faith even in the face of grave danger and then assessing what it would take for you to be able to do so.

Standing for Your Faith

Not many Americans have been asked to stand for their faith in the face of the threat of being persecuted, even killed. However, missionaries and fellow believers around the world are often called on to make such a stand, trusting God for the outcome. This lesson reminds us that our situation could change at any time. Thus people of biblical faith need to stand now for God in the situations we do face as the best way to be ready should we someday face the ultimate challenge of standing firm in the face of the threat of death.

Theophanies of the Old Testament

A *theophany* is an appearance by God in some physical form. The ultimate appearance of God in a physical way is the incarnation, in which the eternal Word of God became a human being—the God-man. Theophanies are appearances of God in the Old Testament. Of course, no one can see the full glory of God and live; but God partially revealed Himself in several ways in the time before the incarnation. One day Abraham saw three men approaching his tent. Abraham recognized one of these as the Lord, who spoke with Abraham and Sarah about

God's promise of a son for them (Gen. 18). God also appeared to others in Old Testament times in the form of a man. At times God appeared in a form other than a human form. God appeared as the angel of the Lord, who is not just any angel. Gideon was visited by this angel, but his conversation with the angel was also described as a talk with the Lord (Judg. 6:12,14). Many people think the angel of the Lord was an Old Testament manifestation of the second Person of the Trinity. Daniel 3:25 tells how Nebuchadnezzar saw a fourth figure in the fiery furnace. Opinions differ about who this person was, but He clearly was a divine figure, as we will see in our comments on 3:25.

❖ *Search the Scriptures*

Nebuchadnezzar made a huge gold statue and ordered all his officials to bow before the statue. He threatened to throw into a burning furnace anyone who refused. Some jealous Babylonian officials reported to Nebuchadnezzar that three of the Jewish officials had not bowed to the statue. These three were Daniel's friends, here called by their Babylonian names: Shadrach [SHAD-rak], Meshach [MEE-shak], and Abednego [uh-BED-nih-goh]. King Nebuchadnezzar had the three brought to him. He asked them if they had worshiped by bowing. The three admitted they had not bowed to the statue. They said they would not bow down and that their God could deliver them if He chose; but in any case, they would not obey the king's order. The furious king had the three men bound and thrown into the furnace. But when the king looked into the furnace, he saw four men walking about. The fourth man looked different from the other three—like a god. Nebuchadnezzar called the three to come out of the furnace, and he praised their God for rescuing them.

Threatening Demand (Dan. 3:1-2,4-6)

What do we know about the image Nebuchadnezzar made? What was his purpose? Who were present? Where was Daniel? Why did the other officials report the three who failed to bow down? What was the punishment for failure to bow down?

Verses 1-2,4-6: **Nebuchadnezzar the king made an image of gold, whose height was threescore cubits, and the breadth thereof six cubits: he set it up in the plain of Dura, in the province of Babylon. 2Then Nebuchadnezzar the king sent to gather together the princes,**

the governors, and the captains, the judges, the treasurers, the counselors, the sheriffs, and all the rulers of the provinces, to come to the dedication of the image which Nebuchadnezzar the king had set up.

[4]Then a herald cried aloud, To you it is commanded, O people, nations, and languages, [5]that at what time ye hear the sound of the cornet, flute, harp, sackbut, psaltery, dulcimer, and all kinds of music, ye fall down and worship the golden image that Nebuchadnezzar the king hath set up: [6]and whoso falleth not down and worshipeth shall the same hour be cast into the midst of a burning fiery furnace.

Nebuchadnezzar made a huge **image of gold** ("gold statue," HCSB). The Hebrew word can mean either "image" or "statue." In chapter 2 the object in Nebuchadnezzar's dream was obviously a statue, but what was it in chapter 3? It was "90 feet high" (HCSB). That is equal to about a nine-floor building. It was a very thin image, for it was only "nine feet wide" (HCSB). Probably this tall, thin image was situated on a large base. Did the tall, thin image look like a person? If so, it was a very skinny figure. Was it more like the Lincoln Memorial with a statue of the president? Or, was it something like our Washington Monument, a huge obelisk dedicated to Washington? Its shape was more like the latter. It was probably gold-plated, not solid gold; but the effect must have been dazzling in the sunlight.

The exact site where the image was erected is unknown, but since it was **in the province of Babylon,** it was probably near the city. Since it was on a **plain,** the tall image would have been seen for miles around. Some people feel the image was inspired by Daniel's interpretation of a gold-headed image in 2:32,35-38. Since the gold head in the dream represented Nebuchadnezzar, the image may represent the king himself. However, since the Babylonian rulers seldom deified themselves, the image probably represented one of his gods. Further support for this is that the word **worship** is used of the image in verses 5 and 7.

Nebuchadnezzar's purpose was more than religious. It was also political. He wanted the dedication of the image to unify his diverse kingdom into one loyal kingdom. The international flavor of those subject to him is seen in verse 4. The people who were there were the various government officials in a province. **The princes** ("satraps," NIV, HCSB) were probably governors of the provinces. The other officers—**the captains, the judges, the treasurers, the counselors,**

the sheriffs—would have been officials of lesser rank in a province. Verse 4 may mean that the people also were there, or it may merely reflect the fact that the officials had come from many countries. The three Jews, for example, were not native Babylonians. Probably Nebuchadnezzar brought captives from other conquered lands.

The signal for people to bow to the image was "the sound of the horn, flute, zither, lyre, harp, drum, and every kind of music" (HCSB). The long list of officials in verse 2 is repeated in verses 3 and 27, and the long list of musical instruments in verse 5 is repeated in verses 7 and 10. "The exact repetition of the list of officials and of the musical instruments may reflect a Semitic style of rhetoric, but the writer succeeds in achieving a satirical effect which may not have been unintentional. Here are all the great ones of the empire falling flat on their faces before a lifeless obelisk at the sound of a musical medley, controlled by the baton of King Nebuchadnezzar."[1]

Of course, Nebuchadnezzar was no comic figure; he was deadly serious about this. During the construction a furnace was used; now it was to serve a new purpose. The king threatened that he would throw **into the midst of a burning fiery furnace** anyone who refused to bow down to the golden image. Nebuchadnezzar, like most absolute rulers, was arrogant and absolutely ruthless. We saw this in his unreasonable and harsh demands of his advisors in 2:7-13, and we see it here with regard to worshiping the image.

What are the lasting truths in Daniel 3:1-2,4-6?

1. The old adage coined by Lord Acton, "Power tends to corrupt, and absolute power corrupts absolutely" is very true.
2. Idol worshipers want others to join in worshiping their idols.
3. People of faith may be tempted to join in various forms of idolatry.

Determined Defiance (Dan. 3:8,12-14)

Why did the Chaldeans report that the Hebrews refused to bow? Did others join the Hebrews' defiance? To what degree were the words of the Chaldeans anti-Semitic? How were their words intended to anger the king? Why did the king allow the three accused men to speak for themselves?

Verses 8,12-14: **Wherefore at that time certain Chaldeans came near, and accused the Jews.**

[12]There are certain Jews whom thou hast set over the affairs of the province of Babylon, Shadrach, Meshach, and Abed-nego; these men, O king, have not regarded thee: they serve not thy gods, nor worship the golden image which thou hast set up. [13]Then Nebuchadnezzar in his rage and fury commanded to bring Shadrach, Meshach, and Abed-nego. Then they brought these men before the king. [14]Nebuchadnezzar spake and said unto them, Is it true, O Shadrach, Meshach, and Abed-nego, do not ye serve my gods, nor worship the golden image which I have set up?

Nebuchadnezzar probably was feeling good. As far as he could see, everyone seemed to be complying. The crowd was so huge that he could not see everyone. About that time, some of the **Chaldeans** reported to him that some had not bowed down to the image. They **accused** ("denounced," NIV) **the Jews.** The word "is literally 'ate the pieces of,' a phrase suggesting severe hatred and bitter language. 'Chewed them up' might be a comparable English idiom, though not as harsh. These astrologers expressed great hostility toward 'the Jews.' Although personal jealousy was likely the primary motive for the astrologers' animosity, anti-Semitism may have been involved."[2] Thus their accusations against Daniel's three friends were similar to those who accused Daniel himself in 6:13. Both groups of accusers were motivated by jealousy and prejudice.

Anti-Semitism is not a modern invention. It is as old as ancient history. It feeds on the distinctiveness of Jewish life based on their religion. Less than a century ago Nazi Germany set a new low point in hatred for Jews. Hitler's speeches and propaganda machine depicted all Jews as an inferior kind of being and as responsible for all Germany's defeats and hard times. This violent hatred reached its ultimate depravity in the Holocaust.

The three accused Jews were Daniel's three friends, here called by their Babylonian names: **Shadrach, Meshach, and Abed-nego.** The accusers reminded Nebuchadnezzar that he had appointed these men to their positions. The accusation was that these men had ignored the king's command by refusing to worship the golden image. Nebuchadnezzar was "in a furious rage" (HCSB) at this report. He was not accustomed to having his orders ignored. To his credit, Nebuchadnezzar did give them an opportunity to speak. He could have taken them directly to the furnace. Did he perhaps recall how pleased he had been with these three in 1:20? In any case, he asked them if the charges against them were true. He even gave them an opportunity to fall down and worship at the time he spoke to them. However, he warned them, "But if you don't worship it, you will immediately be thrown into a furnace of blazing fire—and who is the god who can rescue you from my power" (v. 15, HCSB)?

Were these three the only ones in that vast crowd who failed to bow down? The Bible does not mention anyone else. We wonder if the other Jews bowed down, but if they did, they are not mentioned.

Daniel, who is the key figure in all other chapters of the book, apparently was not at the image episode in chapter 3. A number of guesses about the reason for his absence have been made, but the Bible doesn't tell us. He may have been of such high rank in the government that he was not required to be there. Daniel 2:46-47 reports: "He [Nebuchadnezzar] made him [Daniel] ruler over the entire province of Babylon and chief governor over all the wise men of Babylon. At Daniel's request, the king appointed Shadrach, Meshach, and Abednego to manage the providence of Babylon. But Daniel remained at the king's court" (HCSB). Miller wrote, "His absence may also have been due to other factors, but it is certain that Daniel would never have bowed to the image."[3] Daniel had a horror of any form of idolatry. This was why he determined that he would not drink the king's food and wine in 1:8. If he refused that indirect form of idolatry, he would surely have refused to worship the golden image set up by Nebuchadnezzar.

During the persecution of Christians by the Roman government, accused believers were told that all they needed to do was renounce Christ and offer incense to Caesar. To fail to do this was to be put to death. There are places in today's world where standing up for Christ brings death.

What are the lasting truths in Daniel 3:8,12-14?

1. People's actions, especially those done in public, are observed by others.
2. People who are jealous or prejudiced try to get you in trouble.
3. Anti-Semitism has been around since ancient times. It is a terrible prejudice.
4. Refusing to go along with the crowd can bring criticism and worse.

Confident Defense (Dan. 3:16-18)

What is the meaning of the last part of verse 16? Why is verse 17 hard to translate? How did the three state their faith in what God could do? Why did they not express certainty that God would deliver them? Why does God deliver some but not all? What is meant by the words ***but if not****?*

Verses 16-18: **Shadrach, Meshach, and Abed–nego, answered and said to the king, O Nebuchadnezzar, we are not careful to answer thee in this matter. [17]If it be so, our God whom we serve is able to deliver us from the burning fiery furnace, and he will deliver us out of thine hand, O king. [18]But if not, be it known unto thee, O king, that we will not serve thy gods, nor worship the golden image which thou hast set up.**

These are the key verses in chapter 3. The three accused men began their response to the king with the words, **We are not careful to answer thee in this matter.** On the surface this sounds as if their response was not given with care. Other translations are clearer to people today: "We don't need to give you an answer to this question" (HCSB); "We do not need to defend ourselves before you in this matter" (NIV). There was firmness but no arrogance in their words. They were not going to deny that they were guilty of failing to worship the image, but their words in verses 14-16 took issue with Nebuchadnezzar's question, "Who is that God that shall deliver you out of my hands?" (v. 15).

The first part of verse 17 is hard to translate. The words **if it be so** can be rendered "if we are thrown into the blazing furnace" (NIV) or "if the God we serve exists" (HCSB). The last translation sounds as if the three men doubted God's existence, but surely that is not what they meant. They were trying to respond to the king's cynical question at the end of verse 15. Verse 17 clearly was intended to say that even if the king threw them into the furnace, their God was able to deliver them: **Our God whom we serve is able to deliver us from the burning fiery furnace, and he will deliver us out of thine hand, O king.** Nebuchadnezzar had boasted that no God could take them from being under his power. Shadrach, Meshach, and Abednego testified that their God was able to rescue them and that He would do just that.

The only uncertainty in their reply to the king was expressed in verse 18. Many powerful sermons have been preached on the words **but if not.** The three Jews knew their God was able to deliver them, but they knew He exercises sovereign freedom in whom He chooses to deliver from danger and death. They knew from their study of the Scriptures that God intervenes in history in accordance with His own will, which He had not revealed to the three friends regarding their own fate.

This is one of the deep mysteries of the faith. Since God is able, why does He not always deliver people of faith? We can't explain the many why's of life, but the Scriptures show that the three friends were right. Read Hebrews 11:32-38. Notice that verses 32-35a contain examples of divine deliverances wrought by faith, but that verses 35b-38 list examples of people of faith who were not delivered. The Bible contains examples of conquering faith that led to deliverance and of enduring faith that did not lead to deliverance. Daniel has two examples of conquering faith: the three Hebrew children in the fiery furnace and Daniel in the lion's den. God chose to work miracles in each case. The Bible shows that sometimes faith does not result in earthly deliverance. John the Baptist was beheaded; Stephen was stoned to death; Paul's thorn in the flesh was not taken away. This was not because one group had strong faith and the other had weak faith. It is an issue of God's will.

At the time of verses 16-18, the three young Jews did not know what God would choose to do, but they were willing to leave everything in His hands. They did make one point very strongly—in either case, they would not under any circumstances give in to the king's threats. They told him, **Be it known unto thee, O king, that we will not serve thy gods, nor worship the golden image which thou hast set up.**

What are the lasting truths in Daniel 3:16-18?

1. People of true faith exercise their faith in a God who can do anything.
2. People of true faith trust God to act for good according to His will.
3. And people of true faith resist pressure and threats designed to force them to do something wrong.

Amazing Deliverance (Dan. 3:24-26,28)

How did Nebuchadnezzar respond to the words of Shadrach, Meshach, and Abednego? What was the normal use of the furnace? What shock did the king have when he looked into the furnace? What did he say about the God who delivered the three young men?

Verses 24-26,28: **Then Nebuchadnezzar the king was astonished, and rose up in haste, and spake, and said unto his counselors, Did not we cast three men bound into the midst of the fire? They answered and said unto the king, True, O king. [25]He answered and said, Lo, I see four men loose, walking in the midst of the fire, and**

they have no hurt; and the form of the fourth is like the Son of God.
26Then Nebuchadnezzar came near to the mouth of the burning fiery
furnace, and spake, and said, Shadrach, Meshach, and Abed-nego,
ye servants of the most high God, come forth, and come hither.
Then Shadrach, Meshach, and Abed-nego, came forth of the midst
of the fire.

. . . .

28Then Nebuchadnezzar spake, and said, Blessed be the God of
Shadrach, Meshach, and Abed-nego, who hath sent his angel, and
delivered his servants that trusted in him, and have changed the
king's word, and yielded their bodies, that they might not serve nor
worship any god, except their own God.

Kings do not like to be defied, especially the kind of defiance shown by these three. Nebuchadnezzar had been angry when their failure to bow had first been reported, but that anger was mild compared with his anger after hearing what they said: "Nebuchadnezzar was filled with rage, and the expression on his face changed toward Shadrach, Meshach, and Abednego" (v. 19, HCSB). He issued orders to heat the furnace seven times hotter than normal. He ordered his soldiers to tie up the three men, clothes and all, then to throw them into the furnace. The overheated furnace killed the soldiers when they threw in the condemned men. Nebuchadnezzar was so intent on punishing the Hebrew men that he put his own soldiers in a deadly situation.

Nebuchadnezzar had not constructed the furnace merely for this occasion. It probably was there because it had been used during the construction of the image. Furnaces were important during building projects. They were used to make bricks, smelt ore, melt metal for casting, and heat metal for forging. Now he intended to use it as an execution chamber.

What kind of furnace was it? The Bible says the three condemned men "were cast into the midst of the burning fiery furnace" (v. 21); that they "fell down bound into the midst of the burning fiery furnace" (v. 23); and that the king saw them **walking in the midst of the fire** (v. 25). **Then Nebuchadnezzar came near to the mouth of the burning fiery furnace** and called them to come out. The furnace probably looked like an old-fashioned milk bottle with a smaller entry near the bottom for adding fuel and extracting products. This opening was where the king had stationed himself to view the death of the victims.

But the king saw something he had not expected. He asked his advisors, **Did not we cast three men bound into the midst of the fire?** They agreed that was the case. The awestruck king responded, **I see four men loose, walking in the midst of the fire, and they have no hurt, and the form of the fourth is like the Son of God** ("a son of the gods," NIV, HCSB). Several things about this twist of events astonished the king. First of all, he had expected three helpless burning bodies. Instead, the three condemned men were no longer bound, and they showed no evidence of having been in a fire. Second, they were not only loose, but they were walking about in the flames. The third surprise was the most striking. He saw a fourth figure with them, and the fourth figure looked like someone divine.

Most Bible students would agree with Stephen Miller that "Nebuchadnezzar was polytheistic and had no conception of the Christian Trinity. Thus the pagan king only meant that the fourth figure in the fire was divine. From the Christian perspective, we know that the preincarnate Christ did appear to individuals in the Old Testament. Most likely the fourth man in the fire was the angel of the Lord, God Himself in the person of His Son Jesus Christ."[4]

The Bible is filled with promises such as Isaiah 43:2 that God will be with believers in times of trouble. It is also filled with examples of the Lord's sustaining and sometimes delivering presence in such times. The principle is that whenever we as believers are passing through trials there is another presence with us. We are never alone.

Nebuchadnezzar was impressed by this obvious miracle wrought by the God of the Jews. He expressed his feelings in verse 28. He also was impressed by the tenacity with which the three young men held their ground in spite of his own threats against them. He had felt that his victory over Judah meant that his gods were superior to their God. Now he praised their God for sending **his angel** to deliver His faithful servants. When believers evidence such faith and faithfulness it delivers a strong testimony to unbelievers.

What are the lasting truths in Daniel 3:24-26,28?

1. The Lord's presence is with His people, especially so in times of crisis.
2. Sometimes the Lord delivers His people from what threatens them.
3. Sometimes the Lord sustains but does not deliver His people.
4. God uses the examples and testimonies of faithful believers to soften the hearts of unbelievers.

❖ *Spiritual Transformations*

Nebuchadnezzar built a huge image and commanded all his officials to bow before it and worship. The punishment for disobedience was to be thrown into a burning fiery furnace. Some jealous and prejudiced officials reported to the king that three of his officials—Jews whom the king had appointed—had not bowed and worshiped. The king called Shadrach, Meshach, and Abednego to answer the accusations. The three young men admitted they were guilty as charged. Threatened with being thrown into the furnace, they told the king that their God could deliver them from the furnace if He chose to do so; but in either case, they refused to worship the golden image. The king was enraged by their response. He ordered that the furnace be heated seven times hotter. He ordered his soldiers to bind the three young men and throw them into the furnace. The furnace was so hot that the soldiers were killed when they threw in the prisoners. When the king peered into the furnace, he saw four figures walking around, the fourth being remarkably different. He called the three prisoners to come out, and when they came out, there was no indication they had been in a fire. The king praised the God who performed this miracle and commended the faith and courage of Shadrach, Meshach, and Abednego.

*What does it take to be able to stand up for God and refuse to compromise, even when it is dangerous?*____________________

____

*What qualities do you have or need to be able to demonstrate such courage and commitment?*______________________________

____

Prayer of Commitment: Lord, give me the courage and faith to stand up for You at all times, no matter what the situation. Amen.

[1]Joyce G. Baldwin, *Daniel,* in the Tyndale Old Testament Commentaries [Downers Grove: InterVarsity Press, 1978], 102.

[2]Miller, "Daniel," NAC, 116.

[3]Miller, "Daniel," NAC, 108.

[4]Miller, "Daniel," NAC, 123-124.

Week of September 23

HANDLING SUCCESS SUCCESSFULLY

Background Passage: Daniel 4:1-37
Focal Passage: Daniel 4:4-5,28-37

❖ *Significance of the Lesson*

• The *Life Question* is, Am I too proud for my own good?

• The *Biblical Truth* is that God rejects the proud and blesses the humble.

• The *Life Impact* is designed to help you live for another world in this world by appraising how proud you are and then determining what it would take for you to become humble before the Lord.

When Success Is Dangerous

We have an old adage, "Don't let success go to your head." This adage reminds us that success can be dangerous. In fact, success is at least as big a moral and spiritual danger as failure. Most of us know people who achieve a measure of success and then abandon friends and family and forget God. People of true faith humble themselves and respond to success with gratitude toward God and love for others.

Biblical Warnings Against Pride

C. S. Lewis called pride "The Great Sin." He wrote: "According to Christian teachers, the essential vice, the utmost evil, is Pride. . . . It was through Pride that the devil became the devil; Pride leads to every other vice; it is the complete anti-God state of mind."[1] Pride is the universal sin all have committed. It ignores or rebels against God. It ignores or puts down others. It is deadly to oneself. The Bible is filled with warnings against it. Early in the history of Israel God proclaimed the blessings of obedience and the curses of disobedience. One curse was, "I will break the pride of your power" (Lev. 26:19). As the Israelites prepared to enter the promised land, God warned them against the dangers of success. Moses told them to beware of thinking, "My power and the might of mine hand hath gotten me this wealth." Rather, Moses told them, "Thou shalt remember the LORD thy God: for it is he that giveth thee power to get wealth" (Deut. 8:17-18). The Book of Proverbs says, "Pride goeth before destruction, and a haughty spirit before a fall" (Prov. 16:18). Jesus found pride among His disciples, and tried to call them to humble service rather than rivalry about who was greatest (Mark 10:35-45). Paul found a spirit of pride in early believers and wrote, "For I say, through the grace given unto me, to every man that is among you, not to think of himself more highly than he ought to think" (Rom. 12:3). James wrote, "God resisteth the proud, but giveth grace unto the humble" (Jas. 4:6).

❖ *Search the Scriptures*

During a time of prosperity and complacency, Nebuchadnezzar had a dream that left him frightened and alarmed. A year later he was walking on the flat roof of his palace in Babylon, looking out on the Hanging Gardens and other wonders. He prided himself on his accomplishments, taking the credit for himself. While Nebuchadnezzar was congratulating himself on his accomplishments, a voice from heaven spoke to him in divine judgment, announcing that his kingdom would be taken from him and that he would live like an animal until he acknowledged that the true God is the ruler of kings and kingdoms. All this happened in keeping with the dream he had a year earlier. After a period of time, Nebuchadnezzar turned toward heaven and his sanity returned. He then praised and glorified the true God and acknowledged His sovereignty over people and empires. After this, Nebuchadnezzar's rule over his kingdom was reestablished and even greatly improved. Nebuchadnezzar learned the lesson that God humbles the proud.

Premonition (Dan. 4:4-5)

At what stage in Nebuchadnezzar's life did this event happen? What's wrong with being successful and content? Who was the speaker or writer of this chapter? How did this dream affect Nebuchadnezzar?

Verses 4-5: **I Nebuchadnezzar was at rest in mine house, and flourishing in my palace: 5I saw a dream which made me afraid, and the thoughts upon my bed and the visions of my head troubled me.**

The Greek translation of the Old Testament dates this event in the 18th year of Nebuchadnezzar's reign, but nothing else confirms this date. All we know for sure is that the dream came when Nebuchadnezzar was relaxing and content. Most people think that this event took place fairly late in his reign. Nebuchadnezzar's attitude implies that he was not fighting and had finished many building projects.

Notice the words **I . . . my . . . me.** The speaker in these verses and throughout the chapter (except for vv. 19-33) uses the first person, showing that the speaker was Nebuchadnezzar himself. This is unusual to have a pagan king quoted at length in the Bible. Nebuchadnezzar began chapter 3 with praise to God (vv. 1-3). Then he told us how he got there. **I Nebuchadnezzar was at rest in mine own house, and flourishing in my palace** ("at home in my palace, contented and prosperous," NIV). The first word carries the idea of being at rest or content. The second word means to flourish like a tree. Nebuchadnezzar was as rich as a person could be, and he was contented to the point of being complacent about anything other than himself and his victories and building projects.

What is the difference between *contentment* and *complacency*? *Contentment* is always accompanied by gratitude to God, and it shares with others. *Complacency* is being satisfied with situations that are unsatisfactory to God. It tends to ignore God and the needs of others. Verse 27 is evidence that Nebuchadnezzar was complacent. He took credit for all that he had accomplished.

God sent Nebuchadnezzar the disturbing dream to call him to repent of his pride. Nebuchadnezzar called in his wise men and they could not interpret his dream. At least this time he told them what was in his dream. We wonder why Nebuchadnezzar didn't call in Daniel first, but eventually he called him in and told him his dream. A huge tree stood in the middle of the land. It was beautiful and fruitful. Then a heavenly messenger had the tree cut down, but left its stump. The tree is spoken of as a man, who would live like an animal. The purpose of this was that the man might acknowledge the Most High rules over all.

At first Daniel was reluctant to interpret the dream, but finally he identified Nebuchadnezzar as the tree that was cut down and the man who became like an animal. Daniel promised that Nebuchadnezzar would be restored, but only after acknowledging that God rules. Daniel ended his interpretation with an appeal to Nebuchadnezzar: "Separate yourself from your sins by doing what is right, and from your injustices by showing mercy to the needy" (v. 27, HCSB). This verse clearly shows that the purpose of the disturbing dream was to call Nebuchadnezzar to repent.

God gave Nebuchadnezzar two dreams. In each he had a place of prominence. He was the head of gold in 2:31-32,37-38, and he was the great tree in 4:20-22. The dream in chapter 2 related to all nations and God's eternal kingdom. The dream in chapter 4 related more to Nebuchadnezzar as an individual. In the context of the chapter, it was intended to call the king to repent.

What are the lasting truths in Daniel 4:4-5?

1. Many prosperous and contented people feel they earned what they have and are entitled to enjoy what they have achieved.

2. Not all dreams people have are intended to bring comfort; some are intended to result in repentance.

3. Complacency is not the same as contentment and gratitude.

Pride (Dan. 4:28-30)

How could the king ignore the warning of the dream? At what kinds of things was the king looking as he walked on the roof of the palace? What are some synonyms for the word pride*? Which of the "Biblical Warnings Against Pride" did the king ignore? How does pride distort God, others, and self? Is it wrong to be proud of some things?*

Verses 28-30: **All this came upon the king Nebuchadnezzar. 29At the end of twelve months he walked in the palace of the kingdom of Babylon. 30The king spake, and said, Is not this great Babylon, that I have built for the house of the kingdom by the might of my power, and for the honor of my majesty?**

The dream was striking and Daniel made its meaning clear. How could Nebuchadnezzar ignore the call to repent? He made no response at the time when Daniel called him to repent, and a year later he showed no signs of repentance. To the contrary, he exhibited an exalted view of himself with no reference to God and others. As he looked out on the city of Babylon, he saw all the things that had been built during his reign. There were the famous Hanging Gardens of Babylon, considered one of the wonders of the ancient world. He saw the powerful wall, wide enough for four chariots to ride side by side. He thought of his military victories and remembered that his kingdom included most of the civilized world. These accomplishments were real and worthy of note. The problem was that Nebuchadnezzar said: **Is not this great Babylon, that I have built for the house of**

the kingdom by the might of my power, and for the honor of my majesty?

Verse 30 is the key verse in the lesson. Notice the words **I** and **my.** Nebuchadnezzar took all the credit for all that had been accomplished during his reign. Although he knew about the God of Daniel and on two previous occasions had acknowledged Him (2:46-47; 3:28-29), he did not even mention God in his words of self praise. The word *pride* was not used until 4:37, and it is found in 5:20, where Daniel was reminding Belshazzar what happened to Nebuchadnezzar. Daniel 4:30 is a classic case of pride. It uses the same distorted view seen in Deuteronomy 8:17 that warned the successful not to say, "My power and the might of mine hand hath gotten me this wealth." They needed to "Remember the LORD thy God: for it is he that giveth thee power to get wealth" (Deut. 8:18).

Two aspects of pride make it such a serious sin. Pride takes credit for what only God could do. The Bible emphasizes that the Lord used Nebuchadnezzar to chastise His people. God was the source of Nebuchadnezzar's victories as well as the One who enabled him to build great Babylon. Pride either ignores God or defies Him. Thus it is the ultimate anti-God sin. We respond to the gifts of God by claiming we deserve them and have achieved them on our own. Such proud self-righteousness keeps many people in a life without God and His grace.

Pride also takes all the credit, conveniently forgetting the part played by others. Nebuchadnezzar did not win his battles by himself. He had an army that fought the battles. Nebuchadnezzar did not build all the beautiful buildings in the city; yet he gave no credit to the architects and builders.

As I thought of the word *pride,* I began to think of words that mean the same thing. Here are some of these: vanity, conceit, haughtiness, egotism, arrogance, self-satisfaction, vainglory, boastful, pomposity, self-exaltation, self-centeredness, and ostentation. When we use so many different words to describe pride, it is one evidence that there is a lot of pride around—enough in fact that each of us has some. C. S. Lewis was right when he wrote of pride: "There is one vice of which no man in the world is free; which every one in the world loathes when he sees it in someone else; and of which hardly any people, except Christians, ever imagine that they are guilty themselves."[2]

Are all kinds of pride inherently evil? Is it wrong to be proud of the work you do or of your family? These are good feelings if these things do not keep us from God and His grace and if they are not looked upon in a competitive way. The problem comes when I am proud of my work because I believe it is better than your work or proud of my family because they are better than yours. Again as C. S. Lewis masterfully pointed out: "We say that people are proud of being rich, or clever, or good-looking, but they are not. They are proud of being richer, or cleverer, or better-looking than others."[3] Humility is the opposite of pride. Pride is putting ourselves above others. Humility involves not thinking more highly of yourself than you ought to think (Rom. 12:3).

In his book *Born Again*, Charles Colson tells how he was convicted of the sin of pride as a friend read to him the chapter on the Great Sin by C. S. Lewis. This was the beginning point in his experience of the new birth. Colson wrote: "It was pride—Lewis's 'great sin'—that had propelled me through life. . . . I had been concerned with myself. *I* had done this and that, *I* had achieved, *I* had succeeded and *I* had given God none of the credit, never once thanking Him for any of His gifts to me."[4]

What are the lasting lessons in Daniel 4:28-30?

1. Pride ignores or defies God and takes credit for what God and others have done to help the person.
2. Pride is a sin of which all are guilty.
3. Pride is competitive in claiming to be better than others.

Punishment (Dan. 4:31-33)

How did Nebuchadnezzar learn of his punishment? Why was the punishment so harsh? What was the purpose of the punishment?

Verses 31-33: **While the word was in the king's mouth, there fell a voice from heaven, saying, O king Nebuchadnezzar, to thee it is spoken; The kingdom is departed from thee. 32And they shall drive thee from men, and thy dwelling shall be with the beasts of the field: they shall make thee to eat grass as oxen, and seven times shall pass over thee, until thou know that the most High ruleth in the kingdom of men, and giveth it to whomsoever he will. 33The same hour was the thing fulfilled upon Nebuchadnezzar: and he was driven from men, and did eat grass as oxen, and his body was wet with the dew of heaven, till his hairs were grown like eagles' feathers, and his nails like birds' claws.**

God had given Nebuchadnezzar a year to respond to God's call to repent, but verse 30 shows his impenitent pride. Therefore, as the words of his boast **was in the king's mouth, there fell a voice from**

heaven. The voice told Nebuchadnezzar he had lost **the kingdom.** He was driven out from among a human society and taken into a realm of the wild animals, just as had been foretold by the dream. He ate grass like he was one of the cattle. We are not told how Nebuchadnezzar's family and staff responded to his plight. Perhaps they knew of Daniel's interpretation of the dream. Perhaps Daniel reminded others that the king's condition was not permanent. At any rate, the prophecies of the dream were literally fulfilled.

We are not told exactly how long Nebuchadnezzar lived like a wild animal. Interpreters differ about the meaning of **seven times.** Some think this meant seven years, but others doubt that Nebuchadnezzar's illness lasted that long. Nevertheless, it was long enough to achieve God's purpose that the proud king would learn **that the most High ruleth in the kingdom of men, and giveth it to whomsoever he will.** In spite of all that God had tried to teach Nebuchadnezzar, nothing short of this drastic punishment had taught him this lesson.

The overall lesson is that pride goes before a fall and that God brings down those who lift themselves up with pride. This lesson is taught in Scripture and illustrated abundantly in daily life and in human history. And so for Christians, as Tremper Longman pointed out, there is a warning here too. "Before we pass on, we cannot neglect a warning. While Daniel 4 demonstrates God's ability to humble the arrogant leader of a foreign oppressive empire—an empire 'out there,' so to speak—we must be careful concerning the pride that can infect our own lives. Christians are not immune from a pride that removes our eyes from God and places them squarely on ourselves."[5]

The people who are most proud seldom see their own plight. Hearing the warning that pride goes before a fall, they ask, "What has that got to do with me? I'm not a proud person." Paul had such people in mind when he wrote to proud, self-confident people, "Wherefore let him that thinketh he standeth take heed lest he fall" (1 Cor. 10:12). We are never in greater moral and spiritual peril than when we are blind to our own pride. You may not know when or how your downfall will come, but you can know that it is coming.

What are the lasting truths in Daniel 4:31-33?

1. Pride goes before a fall.
2. Wherever possible, God's purpose is remedial, not merely punitive.
3. Since pride is a universal sin, we all should take this message to heart.

Praise (Dan. 4:34-37)

What was the first step in the king's recovery? What were the components of his prayer? Was his prayer the prayer of a converted man?

Verses 34-37: **And at the end of the days I Nebuchadnezzar lifted up mine eyes unto heaven, and mine understanding returned unto me, and I blessed the most High, and I praised and honored him that liveth forever, whose dominion is an everlasting dominion, and his kingdom is from generation to generation: [35]and all the inhabitants of the earth are reputed as nothing: and he doeth according to his will in the army of heaven, and among the inhabitants of the earth: and none can stay his hand, or say unto him, What doest thou? [36]At the same time my reason returned unto me; and for the glory of my kingdom, mine honor and brightness returned unto me; and my counselors and my lords sought unto me; and I was established in my kingdom, and excellent majesty was added unto me. [37]Now I Nebuchadnezzar praise and extol and honor the King of heaven, all whose works are truth, and his ways judgment: and those that walk in pride he is able to abase.**

Verse 34 is a key verse: "I, Nebuchadnezzar, looked up to heaven, and my sanity returned to me" (HCSB). This validated the promise of Daniel as he interpreted the dream, "Your kingdom will be restored to you as soon as you acknowledge that Heaven rules" (v. 26, HCSB). This moment in Nebuchadnezzar's life reminds us of the moment when the prodigal son came to himself and decided to return to his father (Luke 15:17-19).

Verses 34b-35 record the king's words of praise to God. He praised the sovereign God whose actions are beyond challenge. Then he told of his restoration as king (v. 36). He said, "Now I, Nebuchadnezzar, praise, exalt, and glorify the King of heaven, because all His works are true and His ways are just. And He is able to humble those who walk in pride" (v. 37, HCSB).

Bible interpreters struggle with the issue of whether verses 34-37 represent the prayer of a person who was converted. Edward J. Young wrote: "Calvin denied the conversion, and in this he has been followed by Hengstenberg, Pusey and Keil. The matter is difficult to determine and perhaps cannot be determined. Nevertheless, there are certain considerations which would lead to the conclusion that the king did, after all, experience in his heart the regenerating grace of God.

(1) There is discernible a progress in his knowledge of God. Compare 2:47 with 3:28 and finally with 4:34,35.

(2) The king acknowledges the utter sovereignty of God with respect to his own experience (4:37b).

(3) The king utters true statements concerning the omnipotence of the true God (4:34,35).

(4) The king would worship this God, whom he identifies as King of heaven (4:37a). These reasons lead me to believe that, although the faith of Nebuchadnezzar may indeed have been weak and his knowledge meager, yet his faith was saving faith, and his knowledge true."[6]

What are the lasting truths in Daniel 4:34-37?

1. Restoration begins when one humbles himself or herself by looking up to heaven.
2. One has defeated pride when one truly praises God as the Sovereign of heaven and earth.

❖ *Spiritual Transformations*

Nebuchadnezzar, king of Babylon, had a disturbing dream that proved to be a premonition of bad times to come. When his wise men couldn't interpret the dream, the king called in Daniel. The king committed the sin of pride as he walked on the rooftop of his palace. He expressed pride in the victories he had won and in the city he had built. He ignored any contribution by God and others. As he spoke his boastful words, the judgments in the dream befell him. He became like a wild animal living in the world of animals. His punishment was fitting to his sin, but it had a redemptive purpose. When he looked up to heaven, he was restored, having learned that God is sovereign and that pride leads to punishment.

What are some indicators of pride in the lives of Christians? Add others to this list. Check those that are in your own life.

___ Failure to pray.
___ Taking the credit for achievements.
___ Considering yourself better than others.
___ Failure to praise God.
___ Letting your successes make you proud.
___ Blaming God and others for your failures.

What can you do to deal with the sin of pride and its threat to you and others? ______________________________

Prayer of Commitment: Lord, save me from the sin of pride and help me be loving and humble. Amen.

[1]C. S. Lewis, *Mere Christianity* [New York: The Macmillan Company, 1958], 94.

[2]Lewis, *Mere Christianity*, 94.

[3]Lewis, *Mere Christianity*, 95.

[4]Charles Colson, *Born Again* [Grand Rapids: Baker Book House, 1995], 114.

[5]Tremper Longman, III, *Daniel*, in The NIV Application Commentary [Grand Rapids: Zondervan Publishing House, 1999], 128.

[6] Edward J. Young, *The Prophecy of Daniel* [Grand Rapids: William B. Eerdmans Publishing Company, 1949], 113-114.

Week of September 30

READING THE HANDWRITING ON THE WALL

Background Passage: Daniel 5:1-31
Focal Passage: Daniel 5:1-6,22-28,30-31

❖ *Significance of the Lesson*

• The *Life Question* is, Do I take too casual an approach toward the things of God?

• The *Biblical Truth* is that God evaluates and judges how people live their lives. He weighs their attitudes and actions toward that which is sacred, and He judges them accordingly.

• The *Life Impact* is designed to help you live for another world in this world by examining how secularized you have become and whether you are glorifying God with your life and then deciding how your life could better honor and glorify God.

Sacred and Secular

The English word *sacred* refers to things associated with God and/or things holy. *Secular* refers to things of this world. The biblical terminology for that which is sacred is the Hebrew *qadosh* (and related words) and the Greek *hagios* (and related words). These words refer to that which is "set apart" to God. The biblical terminology in the New Testament for secular are the words *kosmos* ("worldly") and *epigeios* ("earthly"). None of these words is in Daniel 5, but the king and his guests drank wine at a drunken feast using the gold and silver vessels their armies had taken from the temple of the Lord in Jerusalem. This was a secular, profane use of what had been set apart as sacred and holy to the Lord. Some people in our society have no respect for anything sacred or holy, and thus they live only for things of this world. This approach to life is sometimes called "secularism" or "secular humanism." But even for many others, their definition of sacred is not broad enough to cover all that God has set apart for human needs and God's glory. For example, marriage is more than a secular contract; it is a divine commitment. The same is true of parenthood and all aspects of family life. One of the biblical truths rediscovered by the

Protestant Reformation is that daily work—when done consistently with divine purposes—is a sacred calling. Thus the secularization of our society is broader than a mere disregard or disrespect for God, the church, the Bible, and godly living. It also includes failing to recognize God and His gifts in the more commonplace aspects of our lives.

❖ *Search the Scriptures*

King Belshazzar [bel-SHAZ-uhr] held a great banquet. Under the influence of alcohol, he ordered that the vessels King Nebuchadnezzar had taken from the temple in Jerusalem be brought out and used in the revelry. While drinking from these sacred vessels, those at the party praised their pagan gods. In the midst of this debauchery, part of a hand appeared and began writing on the banquet hall wall. As Belshazzar saw this, he turned pale, became terrified, and collapsed. Daniel reminded Belshazzar that he knew about what had happened to Nebuchadnezzar, but he had acted with the same kind of arrogant pride. Therefore, the handwriting on the wall informed Belshazzar that he was guilty before God and that he and his kingdom would come to an end that night.

Secularizing the Sacred (Dan. 5:1-4)

Who was Belshazzar? Was he Nebuchadnezzar's son? Was he a king? Why did he give a great banquet at that time? Why did he order the vessels from the Jewish temple to be brought in? Did his drunken condition excuse what he did? In what ways do people misuse sacred things today?

Verses 1-4: **Belshazzar the king made a great feast to a thousand of his lords, and drank wine before the thousand. [2]Belshazzar, whiles he tasted the wine, commanded to bring the golden and silver vessels which his father Nebuchadnezzar had taken out of the temple which was in Jerusalem; that the king, and his princes, his wives, and his concubines, might drink therein. [3]Then they brought the golden vessels that were taken out of the temple of the house of God which was at Jerusalem; and the king, and his princes, his wives, and his concubines, drank in them. [4]They drank wine, and praised the gods of gold, and of silver, of brass, of iron, of wood, and of stone.**

Not many years ago skeptics did not believe Belshazzar was a real person. At that time, no record of his name had been found, except in the Bible. Then ancient inscriptions were found that mentioned his name. These ancient inscriptions show clearly that Belshazzar was a real person.

Skeptics now focus on two other questions: Was Belshazzar a king? And was he the son of Nebuchadnezzar? In the *King James Version* of Daniel 5 it says he was a king and the son of Nebuchadnezzar. But the ancient inscriptions seem to cast doubt on both of these statements. Let's look more closely at these two questions. The events of Daniel 5 took place in 539 B.C., many years after Nebuchadnezzar had brought Daniel and the sacred temple vessels to Babylon in 605 B.C. After a long reign, the great conqueror Nebuchadnezzar died in 539 B.C. He was succeeded by his son Evil-merodach [EE-vihl-mih-ROH-dak]. The Bible itself bears witness to this in 2 Kings 25:27. After a short reign he was followed by a couple of weak rulers. The last strong king of Babylon was Nabonidus [nab-uh-NIGH-duhs], who was not a descendant of Nebuchadnezzar but perhaps was married to a daughter of the great king. If so, Belshazzar was their son. In those days the word *son* did not always mean a first-generation son. Instead, the word was used of any physical descendant. Thus Belshazzar could have been the grandson of the great king. Any ancestor could be called a "father" in the ancient writings. The *Holman Christian Standard Bible* translates the word for **father** as "predecessor" and the word for *son* as "successor."

Belshazzar also was called a **king.** The records do not give him the title of king, but they show that he was exercising kinglike duties in the city of Babylon, though in a subordinate role to that of his father Nabonidus, who had gone away to fight the armies of the Medes and the Persians that threatened to overthrow the Babylonian Empire. Nabonidus was a captive of the invaders by the time of Belshazzar's feast. In fact, the city of Babylon was under siege at that very time—and even captured that very night. Thus for a while Belshazzar exercised the duties of a king, but not a very wise one.

Belshazzar chose this time to have **a great feast** for **a thousand of his lords.** Such huge feasts were not unknown in ancient times. Esther 1 tells of a similar feast held by the Persian king years after Belshazzar's feast. The Persian feast continued for six months. The feasts had one thing in common—wine flowed freely. At his feast Belshazzar set the pace by drinking wine in front of his guests. The word **tasted** means more than a taste or sip; it referred to him being drunk. This feast was attended not only by the men but also by the women—**his wives, and his concubines.**

Why would Belshazzar have a great feast if the enemy army was near-by? Several theories have been proposed. It may have been a feast scheduled for this time every year. It could have been an act of bravado to show their enemies they did not fear them. After all, the entire city was considered impregnable. The walls were high and thick. A river ran through the city, assuring a water supply in case of a siege. A third theory is that the people had heard that Nabonidus had been defeated and captured and the feast was to honor their new king.

Why did Belshazzar decide to use **the golden and silver vessels** from **the temple** at **Jerusalem**? We are not told. He was no doubt influenced by his drunken condition. Perhaps he wanted to impress his guests. Whatever his reasons may have been, Belshazzar committed a sin that even by pagan standards was considered sacrilegious. By biblical standards it was the worst kind of sin. Then the king added to his sin when he used these sacred vessels and **praised the gods of gold, and of silver, of brass, of iron, of wood, and of stone.**

We want to ask Belshazzar, "Is there nothing you consider sacred? You have taken the vessels that were set apart for the worship of the one true God, and you and your drunken guests have desecrated these holy vessels by drinking from them at your pagan, drunken orgy." People today do things comparable to what Belshazzar did. We want to ask them, "Is there nothing sacred for you?" They take the sacred things designed for God's glory and human needs and they misuse and abuse them.

The Ten Commandments identify some of the sacred things that are used in profane ways. The Third Commandment, for example, sanctifies the name and thus the person of God. Yet the name of God is taken in vain and profaned all the time. A few years ago a surprised person would not say, "Oh my God," but that is standard nowadays. The Fourth Commandment sets aside one day in seven as the Lord's Day, but the majority of people use the day as if it belongs to them to do as they please. The Fifth Commandment speaks of honoring parents. This relationship is intended to be sacred, but many parents and many children disregard this sacred relationship. The Sixth Commandment emphasizes the sanctity of human life, but this sacred gift for the living and the unborn is trampled upon. The Seventh Commandment condemns adultery, but our society condones this breaking of a sacred covenant. Marriage is viewed as a contract not as a sacred commitment.

One way to describe this condition is to call it the secularization of society. The purely secular person lives as though there is no God and, therefore, nothing is sacred. The Bible gives some examples of people like this. Esau is called a "profane person" in Hebrews 12:16. He traded his birthright for a bowl of stew. He was a man of this world. The merchants of Amos 8:4-6 were secular men. They were impatient when holy days interrupted their business, in which they sold inferior goods at inflated prices. The rich farmer of Luke 12:16-21 was a secular man.

One Easter morning I was driving toward church. I passed a filling station owned by the husband of one of the church members. Invitations to church were rejected and ignored by this man. Now there he sat outside his place of business, while his wife and children joined the many who were headed toward the place of worship of the risen Lord. For him, however, it was just another day. As I saw him, I wondered if there was anything sacred in his life.

Some of those who claim to honor sacred things actually dishonored the truly sacred things. Jeremiah 7 condemns people who committed serious sins and then came to the temple, thinking that attendance at the temple covered their sins. The Lord accused them of trying to use the temple the way robbers use their hideouts. They go out and sin; then they come to the temple where they claim to be safe.

When the Lord called Moses, he used a burning bush. As Moses drew near, the Lord told him to take off his sandals because he was standing on holy ground. Then He called Moses to a mission to help people. Some people never think of the ground on which they stand as being holy. They have no sense of the presence of the holy God or of a calling to meet the needs of people. They limit what is holy to certain times and places. They fail to see God calling them to be set apart by and for Him. Many people restrict their definition of holy and sacred to the religious professionals, who form the clergy. Martin Luther and other reformers emphasized that every calling is a sacred calling. Daily work is a holy calling. Failing to see this is to miss what God considers sacred and holy.

What are some lasting truths in Daniel 5:1-4?

1. Pride, idolatry, revelry, orgies, blasphemy, defiance, sacrilege, desecration, and drunkenness characterize those who take no note of what is sacred.

2. When people are under the influence of alcohol, they are emboldened to do foolish things, things that are forbidden or things that they otherwise might not do. Further, alcohol prevents people from seeing their true condition.

3. People who have secularized the sacred do not care if they profane holy things; indeed, they are defiant in purposely doing so.

4. Some people have too limited a view of what God considers sacred. They confine the sacred to certain people and places and fail to see God's holy calling in their daily lives.

The Handwriting on the Wall (Dan. 5:5-6)

What did Belshazzar see on the wall? How did he respond? Who suggested that he call Daniel? How had Belshazzar failed to learn the lessons of history? What were his sins?

Verses 5-6: **In the same hour came forth fingers of a man's hand, and wrote over against the candlestick upon the plaster of the wall of the king's palace: and the king saw the part of the hand that wrote. [6]Then the king's countenance was changed, and his thoughts troubled him, so that the joints of his loins were loosed, and his knees smote one against another.**

In the same hour probably means "at that moment" (HCSB) or "suddenly" (NIV). In other words, while Belshazzar was drinking from the sacred vessels and praising idols, he suddenly saw something that struck terror into his mind and heart. He saw the **fingers of a man's hand.** The fingers were writing something **upon the plaster of the wall of the king's palace.** In uncovering the palace in which they probably were, archaeologists found part of a plaster wall. Some feel that this was the very wall on which Belshazzar saw the hand writing. The bodiless hand was writing **over against the candlestick** ("next to the lampstand," HCSB); therefore, it was easy to see. The king was not the only one who saw it. Later, when Daniel arrived, the message written by the hand was clearly visible.

Belshazzar was very drunk by this time, but the hand writing on the wall attracted his attention and he was terrified—**the king's countenance was changed, and his thoughts troubled him, so that the joints of his loins were loosed, and his knees smote one against another.** Anyone who has been suddenly and seriously frightened knows these feelings. From the Bible's point of view, the handwriting on the wall was designed to convict him of his sins. Some people claim that they would repent if God revealed Himself as clearly as He did in ancient times. God does not cause most of us to see a literal hand writing a message on the wall, but He does give us moments of truth when we can see things as they are.

The terminology of this incident has become part of our language. We say, "He saw the handwriting on the wall." People know that this means that something has forced the person to see the consequences of his actions. We do not literally see handwriting on the wall, but we all can read God's inspired words in the sacred Scriptures. How some people treat the sacred Word reflects the secular mind-set that ignores or rejects what is in the Bible.

The king and his guests raised such a commotion that the "queen came to the banquet hall" (v. 10, HCSB). Who was she? She was not one of the wives of Belshazzar because they were already at the feast (vv. 2-3). The king had followed the example of Nebuchadnezzar in seeking an interpretation from "the mediums, Chaldeans, and astrologers" (v. 7, HCSB). None of them could interpret the writing on the wall. The queen was probably the queen mother (the wife of Nabonidus, the mother of Belshazzar, and possibly the daughter of Nebuchadnezzar). She reminded the distraught king how Daniel had come to Nebuchadnezzar's aid when he needed someone to explain his dreams. She recommended that the king call for Daniel, who was by now a very old man.

What are some lasting truths in Daniel 5:5-6?

1. God uses various ways to confront sinners with the guilt of their sins.

2. Those who have neglected, rejected, or ignored the sacred things of God become weak and afraid when confronted by the hand of God.

Weighed and Found Wanting (Dan. 5:22-28,30-31)

What sin is condemned in verse 22? Why did God send the handwriting on the wall? What words were written? What was their literal meaning? What did Daniel interpret the words to mean? How did the enemy get inside Babylon? Why did God allow judgment to come so quickly?

Verses 22-28: **And thou his son, O Belshazzar, hast not humbled thine heart, though thou knewest all this; 23but hast lifted up thyself against the Lord of heaven; and they have brought the vessels of his house before thee, and thou, and thy lords, thy wives, and thy concubines, have drunk wine in them; and thou hast praised the gods of silver, and gold, of brass, iron, wood, and stone, which see not, nor hear, nor know: and the God in whose hand thy breath is, and whose are all thy ways, hast thou not glorified: 24Then was the part of the hand sent from him; and this writing was written.**

[25]And this is the writing that was written, MENE, MENE, TEKEL, UPHARSIN. [26]This is the interpretation of the thing: MENE; God hath numbered thy kingdom, and finished it. [27]TEKEL; Thou art weighed in the balances, and art found wanting. [28]PERES; Thy kingdom is divided, and given to the Medes and Persians.

God named a new sin and added it to the other sins of which Belshazzar was guilty. Belshazzar failed to learn the lessons of history. He knew the story of what happened to Nebuchadnezzar in chapter 4. He knew how the haughty king had taken credit for all his accomplishments. He knew pride was his downfall. He knew he became insane and lived like an animal until he looked up and God restored him. When Daniel arrived, he added to the list of Belshazzar's sins the sin of pride. Belshazzar knew what had happened to Nebuchadnezzar because of his great pride, but he had learned nothing from this. He was guilty not only of drunkenness, blasphemy, and idolatry but also of egotistical pride. He was so proud that he used the sacred temple vessels to drink wine at his feast. Pride is a besetting sin for sinful humanity. It sets people up in positions that cause them to sin against God in basic ways.

The last part of verse 23 is a description of the consequences of the sin of pride. "You have not glorified the God who holds your life-breath in His hand and who controls the whole course of your life" (HCSB). What a description this is of how God gives and controls our life's breath! He holds our life's breath in His hand, and He controls the whole course of our lives. The folly of sin is its failure to recognize these realities. In our pride we think we control our life's breath and its course.

Verse 24 says that the purpose of the handwriting on the wall was to reinforce these truths. Daniel saw the words that had been written. They were not in some foreign or unknown tongue. Everyone in the room—the king, his guests, his advisors, his mother—all recognized the words, but they did not understand what they meant or how they were to be interpreted. The words were **MENE, MENE, TEKEL, UPHARSIN.** "The three terms, *Mene, Tekel,* and *Parsin* (the 'u' of *Upharsin* of the KJV and RV is 'and') were meaningful to readers of Hebrew and Aramaic and did not represent some strange tongue, as they do for most modern readers. For the king the difficulty was not to give the 'dictionary definition' of the terms, but to see what significance they had for him."[1]

On one level, these words represented different weights and thus coins of different values. According to this view, the first word was the *maneh* (Ezra 2:69; Ezek. 45:12). The second word stood for the Hebrew *shekel.* The third word stood for a half, referring to a half-*maneh.* One view is that the *maneh* or *mina* (of greatest value) stood for Nebuchadnezzar. The shekel (of far less value) was Belshazzar. The half-mina stood for the Medes and Persians. A literal translation would be "mina, mina, shekel, and a half." These words are not only nouns but can be used as verbs. They are used here as passive participles to which Daniel gave a double meaning: "numbered, numbered, weighed, and divided."

Daniel explained the meaning of each of the three words. **MENE; God hath numbered thy kingdom, and finished it. TEKEL; Thou art weighed in the balances, and art found wanting. PERES; Thy kingdom is divided, and given to the Medes and Persians.**

Numbered might imply that their kingdom was predetermined to be finished. Like all human lives and institutions, both Belshazzar and his kingdom had days that were numbered. But Belshazzar was responsible for his fate. God had **weighed** him in the divine scales, and he was seen as a hollow man with little or no substance to him. The third word spoke of the certainty of divine judgment. These three words signified the past, present, and future for Belshazzar. During the past he had been given time to honor God, but he had not done so. Therefore, in the present he was judged and condemned. The judgment would fall that very night. His time had run out. The handwriting may have offered one last chance to repent, but Belshazzar did not repent. He tried to honor Daniel and failed to honor God.

Verses 30-31: **In that night was Belshazzar the king of the Chaldeans slain. 31 And Darius the Median took the kingdom, being about threescore and two years old.**

The Greek historian Herodotus tells how the Persians temporarily diverted the course of the Euphrates River and thus gained access to the city of Babylon when a feast was going on. The Greek historian Xenophon recorded a similar story but added that the Persians killed the Babylonian king, a riotous, indulgent, cruel, and godless young man. In Daniel 1–4 we have four stories about Nebuchadnezzar. In each one he is challenged by the Lord; and in spite of delays, he eventually praised God. Thus in a sense the four stories have happy endings. This is not the case in chapter 5. It ends with judgment on Belshazzar.

Probably even when Belshazzar heard Daniel's interpretation of the handwriting on the wall, he did not realize that his number was up. Final judgment often takes people unawares because they think they still have plenty of time.

What are some lasting truths in Daniel 5:22-28,30-31?

1. When people face a major crisis, they often call for someone who can speak a word from the Lord.
2. God still can use older believers to speak for Him.
3. Sometimes the word from the Lord is a word of judgment.
4. All our days are numbered, which means each day is significant.
5. Many people have no substance to their lives.
6. Judgment often comes in unexpected ways and at times when people are not ready.

❖ *Spiritual Transformations*

Belshazzar, a descendent of his predecessor Nebuchadnezzar, held a huge feast at which he became drunk on the wine he drank. In this condition, he sent for the gold and silver vessels that Nebuchadnezzar had taken years earlier from the temple of the Lord in Jerusalem. Belshazzar committed sacrilege by using these vessels to drink wine at a drunken party. Suddenly the fingers of a man's hand appeared and began writing on the plaster wall of the palace. Belshazzar turned pale and shook with fear. The queen mother told him to call in Daniel, who had interpreted dreams for Nebuchadnezzar. When Daniel arrived, he interpreted the handwriting on the wall. Belshazzar's days were numbered, he was judged and found wanting, and God's judgment was coming. That night Belshazzar died when the Medes and Persians conquered Babylon.

Here is a list of sacred things. Evaluate how well you honor sacred things. Beside each item, write a number with 1 for lowest and 10 for highest.

Holy Name	____	Your job	____
Holy Book	____	Your marriage	____
Holy People	____	Your family	____
Lord's Day	____	Your tithe	____

How can you do a better job of honoring holy things? ____________

____

Prayer of Commitment: Lord, You are holy. Help me to glorify everything You have set apart as holy. Amen.

[1]Baldwin, *Daniel*, 123.

Study Theme

Believer's Handbook 101

John R. W. Stott introduced his commentary on the Sermon on the Mount with the words, "The Sermon on the Mount is probably the best-known part of the teaching of Jesus, though arguably it is the least understood, and certainly it is the least obeyed. It is the nearest thing to a manifesto that He ever uttered, for it is His own description of what He wanted His followers to be and to do. To my mind no two words sum up its intention better, or indicate more clearly its challenge to the modern world, than the expression 'Christian counter-culture'."[1]

Stott explained that what Jesus taught in Matthew 5–7 is the opposite of the secular culture and also of the religious culture of the scribes and Pharisees. For example, Jesus began with the Beatitudes, which say that God approves people who are poor in spirit, who mourn, and who are meek. These and the other Beatitudes are contrasts to the world's ways. Jesus called His disciples, a small group of ordinary men, the salt of the earth and the light of the world. Jesus claimed to fulfill the Old Testament and proceeded to show how different His ways were from the rules of the scribes and Pharisees.

This week we begin a two-month study of the Sermon on the Mount. In the first part Matthew 5 will be studied. The first lesson, "Quality Is Job One," is based on verses 1-12. This is the Beatitudes. The second lesson, "High-Impact Believers," is based on verses 13-20. These verses contain Jesus' call for His followers to be light and salt and the necessity to have a better standard of righteousness than the religious leaders. The third lesson, "The Heart of the Matter," is based on verses 21-32. Here Jesus taught about murder, adultery, and divorce, emphasizing that His way looked behind actions to attitudes. The fourth lesson, "R-E-S-P-E-C-T—Find Out What It Means," is based on verses 33-48. These verses deal with what Jesus taught about honesty, retaliation, and love for enemies.

[1]John R. W. Stott, *The Message of the Sermon on the Mount,* in The Bible Speaks Today [Downers Grove: InterVarsity Press, 1978], 15.

Week of October 7

QUALITY IS JOB ONE

Bible Passage: Matthew 5:1-12

❖ *Significance of the Lesson*

- The *Life Question* is, What foundational qualities characterize a believer's life?
- The *Biblical Truth* is that believers demonstrate qualities of the blessed Christian life.
- The *Life Impact* is designed to help you follow Jesus and live according to His teachings by describing foundational qualities of a believer's life and then expressing qualities in which you intend to grow.

Blessed by God

Many Christians, especially those in the United States, do not understand what it means to be blessed by God. They equate ease, comfort, and material abundance with divine blessings. As Jesus began His Sermon on the Mount, He highlighted a number of qualities, the possessors of which He called blessed. Contrary to popular culture and opinion today, the qualities He elevated would not generally be regarded as positive or desirable. Thus today's adults need to understand the blessed life from Jesus' perspective.

Word Study: *Blessed*

Blessed is the key word in the Beatitudes. The Greek word is *makarios.* The word can mean "blessed," "fortunate," and "happy." Some Bible students translate the word as "happy," assuming that it points to characteristics of a happy life. Others don't think this was Jesus' point. They think the Beatitudes do not represent a divine formula for human happiness but look at humanity from God's perspective. These are the kind of people who are in God's kingdom and will be in His future kingdom. Such people are happy, but that is because they are the kind of people blessed by God.

❖ *Search the Scriptures*

Jesus' disciples came to Him and He taught them. Jesus pronounced as blessed those disciples who were poor in spirit, who mourned, who were meek, who hungered and thirsted after righteousness, who were merciful, who were pure in heart, who were peacemakers, and who were persecuted for righteousness' sake. He addressed the persecuted and told them to rejoice because of their great reward in heaven.

Learn from Jesus the Teacher (Matt. 5:1-2)

What had Jesus been doing prior to these verses? Was His primary audience His disciples or the crowds? Why is the Sermon on the Mount called an ethic of grace?

Verses 1-2: **And seeing the multitudes, he went up into a mountain: and when he was set, his disciples came unto him: [2]and he opened his mouth, and taught them, saying,**

Matthew 4:23-25 states that Jesus had been preaching, teaching, and healing throughout Galilee. News about Him spread and great crowds flocked to Him. Matthew 5:1 indicates that Jesus responded to this by going **up into a mountain.** The reference could be to one of the hills around Capernaum. We don't know the specific mountain, but this was an attempt to withdraw to teach **his disciples**, who **came unto him.** Jesus sat down **and taught them.** Sitting was the normal posture for teachers in Jesus' day.

So what about **the multitudes**? Did Jesus focus this teaching on them or on His disciples or on both? The context of the passage and the content of the teaching seem to identify the word **them** with the disciples, not with the crowds. Verse 1 does not indicate whether some of the crowds were present when Jesus did the teaching. Matthew 7:28 shows that some from the crowds were there at the conclusion of the sermon. Therefore, it is logical to assume that some of the crowds were present and heard what Jesus said. However, the focus of this teaching was to His disciples. We know that Jesus already had called Peter, Andrew, James, and John to be disciples (4:18-22). Although Matthew didn't list all 12 apostles until 10:1-4, Jesus probably had them all with Him here.

Occasionally someone will say, "I don't need salvation from sin; I just live by the Sermon on the Mount." I wonder if that person has ever read the Sermon on the Mount. People like that assume the Sermon is a list of rules for conduct that any well-intentioned person can keep. Anyone who seriously reads Matthew 5–7 realizes that this is a false assumption.

Serious readers often go to the other extreme and ask if anyone can live by the Sermon's high standards. This group looks at such moral demands as to love your enemies, give your jacket to someone who just took your coat, and never to have a lustful or an angry thought. How could Jesus expect people to live by such high standards? Various theories have been proposed about the high demands. One theory is that the purpose of the Sermon on the Mount is to convict us of sin and prepare us for salvation because we cannot evidence this kind of righteousness on our own. Another theory is that these high standards are for a future age. A third theory is that these demands can be met by only a handful of people. Many of us see the Sermon as an ethic of grace for committed disciples. We cannot keep all its high demands, but the God of grace enables us to move in their direction.

This is a significant factor in how we interpret Matthew 5–7. The material in these chapters was spoken and written for people who know the Lord. The Sermon on the Mount is for people who have experienced the new birth. "Only a belief in the necessity and the possibility of a new birth can keep us from reading the Sermon on the Mount with either foolish optimism or hopeless despair. Jesus spoke the Sermon to those who were already His disciples and thereby also the citizens of God's kingdom and the children of God's family. The high standards He set are appropriate only to such. We do not, indeed could not, achieve this privileged status by attaining Christ's standards. Rather by attaining His standards, or at least approximating to them, we give evidence of what by God's free grace and gift we already are."[1]

God treats us as His children. He wants nothing for us but the highest and best, but He knows we continue to fall short at some points. He deals with His children with mercy and grace. Those who see this give their best to such a Father. Jesus' sermon is an ethic of grace.

What are the lasting truths in Matthew 5:1-2?

1. The teachings of the Sermon on the Mount are not simple ethical rules that any well-intentioned person can obey.

2. These teachings are for all of Jesus' disciples.

3. God our Father seeks the best from us, forgives us when we fall short, and helps us in the future.

Live the Upside-Down Life (Matt. 5:3-10)

What kinds of people are declared blessed in the Beatitudes? What blessing is given to each? Why do these kinds of people represent "the upside-down life"?

Verses 3-10: **Blessed are the poor in spirit: for theirs is the kingdom of heaven.**

4 Blessed are they that mourn: for they shall be comforted.

5 Blessed are the meek: for they shall inherit the earth.

6 Blessed are they which do hunger and thirst after righteousness: for they shall be filled.

7 Blessed are the merciful: for they shall obtain mercy.

8 Blessed are the pure in heart: for they shall see God.

9 Blessed are the peacemakers: for they shall be called the children of God.

10 Blessed are they which are persecuted for righteousness' sake: for theirs is the kingdom of heaven.

In the Word Study we noted that the word **blessed** *(makarios)* introduces each of the eight Beatitudes. Translators have struggled with the best way to communicate this word. Many believe it refers to being blessed by God. The introduction could be "blessed by God" are the. . . . Other Bible students have championed the idea that *makarios* means "happy." Thus they see these eight things as the divine formula for human happiness. The content and structure, however, is a description of the kind of people who belong to God's eternal kingdom, not a prescription for human happiness. The central issue here is how God evaluates us, not how happy we feel.

Each Beatitude is followed by a clause beginning with the word **for** (*hoti*; "because," HCSB). The clauses describe the blessing given to the specific kind of person. For example, the blessing given to **the poor in spirit** is that **theirs is the kingdom of heaven.** The Beatitudes are unlike the spiritual gifts in which the gifts differ from person to person. "These are not eight separate and distinct groups of disciples, some of whom are meek, while others are merciful and yet others are called upon to endure persecution. They are rather eight qualities of the same group who at one and the same time are meek and merciful, poor in spirit and pure in heart, mourning and hungry, peacemakers and persecuted."[2] Stott continued, "Just as the eight qualities describe every Christian (at least in the ideal), so the eight blessings are given to every Christian. True, the particular blessing promised in each case is appropriate to the particular quality mentioned. At the same time it is surely not possible to inherit the kingdom of heaven without inheriting the earth, to be comforted without being satisfied or to see God without receiving His mercy and being called His children. The eight qualities together constitute the responsibilities, and the eight blessings the privileges, of being a citizen of God's kingdom."[3]

Are these blessings present or future? Some are in the future tense; others are not. Like most of the blessings promised in the New Testament, the Beatitudes have both present and future dimensions. The kingdom is already a reality (Luke 17:20-21), and we pray for its future coming (Matt. 6:10).

Are the eight qualities the result of divine grace or human effort? The first one gives an answer. The answer must combine respect for God's sovereign grace and human response. The **poor in spirit** are those who have humbled themselves before God so His grace can do its part. Those who turn to God are not the proud but the humble. People must recognize they are spiritually destitute in order to receive God's grace.

If you look at the qualities advocated in the Beatitudes, you will notice how different they are from the world's way of looking at things. Few people were attracted by the call to be poor of spirit. Even fewer would want to view mourning as a positive thing. And hardly anyone strives to be **meek,** or to believe that the meek **shall inherit the earth.** The world's values and goals are the opposite from the Beatitudes. They are upside down from Christ's way.

Several years ago I was writing on the Sermon on the Mount, and I decided to seek to write a list of the world's beatitudes that was close to how worldly people think and live. Here is what I came up with. Compare it verse-by-verse with the verses in Jesus' Beatitudes.

1. Blessed are the rich and famous, for they will be recognized as important people.
2. Blessed are people who party, for they will enjoy life to the fullest.
3. Blessed are the aggressive, for they will inherit the earth.
4. Blessed are people who do their own thing, for they will find personal fulfillment.
5. Blessed are those who take care of number one, for they don't need to worry about anyone else.
6. Blessed are the wheelers and dealers, for they are winners in this dog-eat-dog world.

7. Blessed are those who do not get involved in other people's problems, for they will not get caught in the middle.
8. Blessed are those who don't rock the boat, for everyone will like them.

The second of Jesus' Beatitudes deals with people who **mourn.** Verse 4 states the proper attitude of people who recognize their spiritual poverty. They mourn their plight and the plight of a world of sinners. This seems to be the primary thrust of the verse, although some people think it also testifies to God's empathy with all who mourn life's inevitable losses. The verse seems to focus on mourning our own sins and for a lost world awaiting deliverance from moral and spiritual darkness.

The promise to those who mourn was that **they shall be comforted.** In Luke 6:25 Jesus pronounced judgment on the complacent rich and frivolous pleasure-seekers, saying, "Woe to you who are laughing now, because you will mourn and weep" (HCSB). But Jesus promised in verse 21: "Blessed are you who weep now, because you will laugh" (HCSB).

Matthew 5:5 stands in the most contrast to the world's viewpoint: **Blessed are the meek: for they shall inherit the earth.** This Beatitude sounds preposterous by the usual human standards. Everyone knows that the aggressive go-getters are the ones who will inherit the earth, and the meek are left out. Jesus was either wrong about this, or He knew something about the meaning of **meek** that we don't know. The word *praus* is often translated "gentle" (HCSB), but a gentle person is still not the kind of person that most people believe will inherit the earth. A closer look at the Greek word reveals a word picture of a gentle horse. He is a powerful animal, but his strength is under control. Jesus used this word to describe Himself (11:29). Many people live as though everything revolves around them. Jesus understood this word of a person who lives in harmony with God, others, and self.

In what sense will the meek inherit the earth? The meek know they will inherit the earth because they expect to inherit what belongs to their Heavenly Father. Most people go through life limiting their inheritance to a little piece of the earth. They clutch it to themselves and say "mine" to anyone who seeks it. God's true people recognize that what God has is theirs.

Verse 6 is the Fourth Beatitude. Jesus could not have chosen stronger images than **hunger and thirst.** The people of Jesus' land and time did not take food and water for granted. Many lived from day to day in a survival stance, and good, safe water was scarce. Most of the common people had known the gnawing agony of real hunger and thirst. When one is truly hungry, the thought of food becomes an all-consuming passion. The same is true of thirst, only death from thirst comes more quickly than starvation. Jesus used these two deep needs to describe how deeply should be our striving for **righteousness.** This word has at least three meanings in the Bible. All could be included in verse 6: (1) salvation through being made right with God, (2) a righteous life made possible by God's Spirit, and (3) standing for right and justice in an evil and unjust world.

God blesses those who seek "first the kingdom of God, and his righteousness" (6:33). The promise to those who hunger and thirst after righteousness is that **they shall be filled.** One of the biblical images of future happiness is the picture of a great feast (Matt. 22:4; Luke 22:18; Rev. 19:9). This may be the image Jesus had in mind when He made the promise in verse 6, but He also promised to satisfy our spiritual hunger and thirst. This happens as we walk with the Lord, and it will be fulfilled in His future kingdom (Rev. 7:14-17).

Generally speaking, the first four Beatitudes deal with our relationship with God and the last four deal with our relationships with others. Verse 7 says that God blesses people who are **merciful.** The biblical concept of mercy has two main categories: (1) pardon or forgiveness for the guilty, and (2) kindness shown to the needy. Because both are prominent in both Testaments, we cannot exclude either category from the Fifth Beatitude. God is the model for both forgiving mercy and helping mercy (Ex. 34:6-7; Jas. 5:11). Because God is merciful to sinners, believers also are to be merciful in forgiving those who hurt us (Matt. 18:23-30). Because God helps the needy, so should we show mercy by helping the needy (Luke 10:30-37).

The promise to the merciful is **they shall obtain mercy.** This would include mercy from others and from God. The Bible teaches that we cannot expect divine forgiveness if we have an unforgiving spirit. Forgiveness is a two-way street. The heart that is open to receive God's forgiveness is open for forgiveness to flow out to others.

The words **pure in heart** can have more than one meaning. Some Bible students see it as single-hearted devotion to God that results in a pure and holy life. Others see it as sincerity toward God and others. A strong case can be made for each view, but since the last four Beatitudes refer to relations with others, the second view gains an edge.

The sincere person is transparent and guileless. With such people, what you see is what you get. The world's wheelers and dealers often have hidden agendas. They thrive on guile and sometimes dishonesty.

The pure in heart are promised that **they shall see God.** Seeing God includes a spiritual awareness of Him, even during our earthly pilgrimage; but the ultimate reward is the future sight of Him: "Now we see but a poor reflection as in a mirror; then we shall see face to face" (1 Cor. 13:12, NIV).

Peacemakers refers to God's representatives in the ministry of reconciliation. They are the royal ambassadors who call sinners separated from God to be reconciled to Him and find peace with God (Rom. 5:1; 2 Cor. 5:20). They promote oneness of spirit among believers who were once separated not only from God but also from one another (Eph. 2:11-22). They seek to bring together believers who have problems with each other (Phil. 4:3). Peacemakers pray for and work to promote peace in all relationships.

Their blessing is that **they shall be called the children of God.** God is the great Reconciler and Peacemaker, and He calls His children to be ministers of reconciliation (2 Cor. 5:18-19). Peacemakers are recognized because they are doing what God does. Peacemaking is risky and costly. God's reconciliation cost the death of His Son. Believers who take the initiative in this costly venture are recognized by many people to be children of the great Peacemaker. This will be even more apparent in the coming kingdom.

The last Beatitude is the divine blessing pronounced on people who **are persecuted for righteousness' sake.** People often react negatively to the kinds of people in the first seven Beatitudes, especially to the work of peacemakers. Those who try to bring peace often end up stirring up the anger of those they seek to reconcile. The world, therefore, advises not to seek to win people to Christ or to seek to bring peace between warring groups. The world puts first its own safety and well-being. When a peacemaker comes along, they see him or her as a threat; therefore, they oppose the peacemaker. Jesus knew that all of the band of disciples He was teaching would face persecution in the future. He wanted them to know that being persecuted for the sake of Christ was a blessed condition.

It is interesting that the first and last Beatitudes have the same blessing. Both **the poor in spirit** and those **persecuted for righteousness' sake** are promised that **the kingdom of heaven** is theirs. This may imply a progression in the Beatitudes that mirrors stages in Christian experience. At least the first describes the kind of humility necessary to enter the kingdom. The last describes the ultimate expression of faith in enduring persecution.

As you have examined each of Jesus' Beatitudes, have you compared it with the world's attitude toward the same subject? Do you see what is meant by "Live the Upside-Down Life"? The Beatitudes and the Sermon on the Mount as a whole turn upside down the world's view of the good life. John Dean was one of president Richard Nixon's staff who served prison time. In his book *Blind Ambition* the first chapter is "Reaching for the Top, Touching Bottom." Dean wrote: "For a thousand days I would serve as counsel to the President. I soon learned that to make my way upward, into a position of confidence and influence, I had to travel downward through factional power plays, corruption and finally outright crimes. . . . Slowly, steadily, I would climb toward the moral abyss of the President's inner circle until I finally fell into it, thinking I had made it to the top just as I began to realize I had actually touched bottom."[4] What the worldly consider to be the top turns out to be the bottom. Christ turned the world's view upside down.

What are the lasting truths in Matthew 5:3-10?

1. The Beatitudes describe the kind of people whom God approves and blesses.

2. Such persons are humble, serious, gentle, righteous, merciful, sincere, peacemakers, and faithful.

3. Their blessings include the kingdom of heaven, comfort, the earth, fulfillment, mercy, seeing God, and being recognized as God's children.

4. These qualities have their source in God's grace and the Spirit's power.

5. The qualities God approves are totally different from the world's values.

Willingly Suffer for Godliness (Matt. 5:11-12)

*Why did Jesus switch to the word **you**? What forms of suffering did Jesus mention? How can we rejoice when we are suffering?*

Verses 11-12: **Blessed are ye, when men shall revile you, and persecute you, and shall say all manner of evil against you falsely, for my sake. [12]Rejoice, and be exceeding glad: for great is your reward in heaven: for so persecuted they the prophets which were before you.**

Jesus addressed the disciples personally and directly by using the word **you.** Perhaps He felt they needed special encouragement to face opposition and persecution. As much as we wish that all people would respond positively to the good news, some reject it and mistreat those who accept it. In verse 10 He spoke of hostility **for righteousness' sake.** In verse 11 He said it was **for my sake.**

Jesus emphasized some of the kinds of persecution to expect. **Men shall revile** ("insult," NIV, HCSB) **you.** Also, they **shall say all manner of evil against you falsely.** The power of words can be good or bad. Persecutors and critics of faith often resort to ridicule and slander.

How did Jesus say His followers are to respond? **Rejoice, and be exceeding glad.** One of the amazing teachings of the New Testament is that joy is not dependent on outward circumstances. In fact, Christians can rejoice in the worst of circumstances (Rom. 5:3-4; Jas. 1:2; 1 Pet. 1:6).

As Jesus' followers they followed in a noble train of **prophets** who were faithful unto death. Thus they also could rejoice, Jesus told them, because **great is your reward in heaven.**

What are the lasting truths in Matthew 5:11-12?

1. Ridicule and slander are forms of persecution if such insults are for Christ's sake.
2. Christians should expect opposition and persecution.
3. Believers can rejoice when they suffer persecution.

❖ *Spiritual Transformations*

Jesus took His disciples onto a mountain to teach them. Some of the crowd probably were there, but Jesus focused the Sermon on the Mount (Matt. 5–7) on His disciples. He listed eight qualities that God blesses and eight blessings. All the qualities and all the blessings apply to every disciple. The qualities He listed are the opposite of the qualities the world considers important. The world considers its own ways to be the top of life when actually they are the bottom. Jesus made the Beatitude on persecution personal. He told His followers to rejoice when they are insulted or slandered because of their faith in Him.

Compare Jesus' Beatitudes with the list of the world's beatitudes. Which of Jesus' Beatitudes do you follow most closely? ____________

*Which do you need the Lord's help with the most?*______________

Prayer of Commitment: Lord, help me to allow Your grace and power to make me the kind of person You approve and bless. Amen.

[1]Stott, *The Message of the Sermon on the Mount*, 29.
[2]Stott, *The Message of the Sermon on the Mount*, 31.
[3]Stott, *The Message of the Sermon on the Mount*, 34.
[4]John Dean, *Blind Ambition* [New York: Simon and Schuster, 1976], 30-31.

Week of October 14

HIGH-IMPACT BELIEVERS

Bible Passage: Matthew 5:13-20

❖ *Significance of the Lesson*

• The *Life Question* is, How can I impact my society for Christ?

• The *Biblical Truth* is that believers impact society for Christ when they help preserve it by their influence, project the light of Christ on it by their good works, and seek to promote godly righteousness within it.

• The *Life Impact* is designed to help you follow Jesus and live according to His teachings by identifying ways you can impact society for Christ and then committing to do so.

Everybody Has Influence

Influence is something everyone has. Some influence is good and some of it is bad; however, all of us have some kind of influence, and all of us are influenced by those about us. Parents are among those who have great influence for good or bad. Teachers also are influencers. Friends influence us and are influenced by us. In fact, someone—or more than one—is looking at you as an example. It is up to you what influence you will have.

Salt in the New Testament World

Salt was a precious commodity in the first century. For our society it is a condiment, a seasoning for food. In ancient times, it was that plus much more. Its great value was as a preserver for meat. Before the days of refrigeration, to avoid spoiling, meat had to be salted. Salt also was used in religious offerings. Hebrew offerings were salted (Lev. 2:13). Salt was often used to pay Roman soldiers; thus arose our saying, "A man should be worth his salt." Our English word *salary* comes from the Latin word *sale*, for salt.

❖ *Search the Scriptures*

Jesus taught His followers to be to society what salt is to meat—to preserve and save it from corruption and to add flavor. Jesus called His followers to be lights in a dark world by letting their good works glorify the Father in heaven. He said that He had come to fulfill the Scriptures, not destroy its teachings. He taught His followers to have a righteousness different from the self-righteous religious leaders.

The three points in the Lesson Outline tells us how as Christians we can impact our society.

Preserve Influence (Matt. 5:13)

Why was this verse a shocking statement? Why was salt so important to that culture? What are evidences the earth needs saving? How can salt lose its ***savor****? What is the source of the description of someone as* ***good for nothing****?*

Verse 13: **Ye are the salt of the earth: but if the salt have lost his savor, wherewith shall it be salted? it is thenceforth good for nothing, but to be cast out, and to be trodden under foot of men.**

The word **ye** ("you," NIV, HCSB) ties these hearers to the same people in verses 11-12. Jesus had just described His people as the kind that worldly people consider "losers"; yet He added that this small persecuted band of ordinary people were **the salt of the earth.** What were some reasons salt was considered valuable in that day? The primary reason was its ability to preserve meat from corruption, but it was also used as a condiment (Job 6:6), a fire catalyst, a fertilizer, an antiseptic, and an element in covenant sacrifices (Num. 18:19). Jesus seems to have had in mind the use of salt to save or preserve meat from spoiling. The four fishermen among the disciples knew this well. They would have been out of business without salt to preserve fish.

Jesus' statement reveals something about the world as well as something about the disciples. The world is being corrupted by sin and death. Paul's description of the sins of first-century Greco-Roman society (Rom. 1:18-32) reveal a society filled with all manner of sins. They had turned from God to the folly of idols. This in turn led to sexual perversion as well as to all kinds of strife. Our society is equally riddled with moral and spiritual corruption. Earthly societies without God are caught in this corrupting process of sin and death.

While He was on earth, Jesus interacted and even befriended people caught in this decaying process. He did not participate in their sins. He was in the world but not of the world. He prayed that His disciples follow Him in this mission. To interact with sinful people believers must have contact with them, just as salt has to be worked into the meat in order to preserve it. But in order to be a saving influence instead a part of the corruption, believers must not be of the world.

Savor means "flavor." Herschel H. Hobbs pointed out that some people criticize Jesus for speaking of salt that loses its savor. They argue that salt never loses its savor. Today we use refined salt; whereas the people of Jesus' land got salt from the Dead Sea, and who knows for sure how impurities affected their salt? Because salt can be dissolved in water, it can be washed out, leaving a white powder that has no good use and may even harm the ground. Thus such salt was used on paths and roads. Hobbs concluded, "Whether or not salt can lose its flavor, Christians can lose theirs."[1] Jesus called professing believers **good for nothing** if they are not being the salt of the earth. If Christians are indistinguishable from the people of this world, they are useless to help preserve their society. The corruptible world will be totally consumed by its sin without the influence of the salt of the earth.

What are the lasting truths in Matthew 5:13?

1. Our world is being corrupted by sin.
2. Believers are to help save a corruptible world.
3. Believers who are not being a preservative influence on their society are useless to the kingdom.

Project Light (Matt. 5:14-16)

In what sense is Jesus the light of the world? In what sense are we? What provided light in a Jewish house? How should believers relate to sinful people? How do we reconcile these verses with Matthew 6:1-8,16-18?

Verses 14-16: **Ye are the light of the world. A city that is set on a hill cannot be hid. [15]Neither do men light a candle, and put it under a bushel, but on a candlestick; and it giveth light unto all that are in the house. [16]Let your light so shine before men, that they may see your good works, and glorify your Father which is in heaven.**

While the disciples were still reeling from the commission to be the salt of the earth, Jesus said, **Ye are the light of the world.** Jesus Himself was called "the light of the world" (John 8:12). He is the source of light; we can only reflect His light. The sun is a source of light. The moon's light is a reflection from the sun. This illustrates the relation between believers as lights and Jesus as the source of light.

Most of us in the age of electricity have no idea how dark it was before modern means of illumination. When the sun set, unless there was a moon, it was pitch black. Those who ventured outside needed torches or lamps. The translations **candle** and **candlestick** reflect later forms of lighting. In Jesus' day, the means of illuminating the night was "a lamp," which was placed on "a lampstand" (HCSB). Each dwelling had a lamp to provide light. The lamps were bowls of oil with wicks that could be lit.

In verse 14 Jesus was saying something about the world and His followers. Just as the world is subject to corruption and disciples are to be the salt of the earth, so is the world lost in the darkness of sin and disciples are to be the light of the world.

The nature of light is to shine. Even a small light can pierce the deepest darkness. Jesus spoke of **a city that is set on a hill.** He said that it **cannot be hid.** Some people think Jesus had Jerusalem in mind, which is on a high mountain. Perhaps He had the words from Isaiah 60:1 in mind: "Arise, shine; for thy light is come, and the glory of the LORD is risen upon thee." Moralists of the day called people to become what they should be; Jesus called us to be what we are—salt and light.

In a dark house, no one lit a lamp and then covered it with a basket. That would defeat the purpose of the light. If hiding one's light is not done in the physical world, Christians should not do it in the spiritual world. A believer who hides his light is like one who has lost his savor.

Instead of hiding your light, you should **let your light** be seen. In Matthew 6:1-8,16-18 Jesus warned against doing good deeds to be seen and praised by people. But here in 5:16 He was talking about letting your good deeds be seen so that others will **glorify your Father which is in heaven.** The passage in chapter 6 warns against doing the right thing for the wrong reason—pride. Matthew 5:16 calls us to do the right things for the right reason—to glorify God. In both cases other people see our good works. The question is, What do they do then? Do they praise you or God? This is one reason why our verbal testimony must give any credit for good in our lives to the Lord. Without such a verbal witness, other people may think only of what a good person you are.

The Dead Sea Scrolls revealed a community of people who withdrew from secular society to form a community who lived devout and holy lives. They called themselves "sons of light." They viewed their mission differently from what Jesus called His followers to be and do. Jesus did not withdraw from life but involved Himself so much in life that His commitment led to the cross. He also called His followers to be in but not of the world (John 17:14-18). To be of the world is to compromise with it and become like it. Professing Christians who don't allow God's light to shine through them are as useless and as dangerous as salt that has lost its savor. They are of no use in shining in the darkness. And the sin-darkened world is left to grope in darkness.

What are the lasting truths in Matthew 5:14-16?

1. Jesus is the ultimate light of the world.
2. Jesus calls His disciples to reflect His light.
3. We live in a sin-darkened world.
4. As believers, we are to live an openly Christian life, which glorifies God, not us.

Promote Righteousness (Matt. 5:17-20)

*Why would anyone accuse Jesus of destroying **the law** or **the prophets**? To what do these words refer? In what ways did Jesus fulfill them? How did the people regard **the scribes and Pharisees**? How did Christ's definition of **righteousness** differ from theirs? What principle of biblical interpretation is suggested by these verses?*

Verses 17-20: **Think not that I am come to destroy the law, or the prophets: I am not come to destroy, but to fulfill. [18]For verily I say unto you, Till heaven and earth pass, one jot or one tittle shall in no wise pass from the law, till all be fulfilled. [19]Whosoever therefore shall break one of these least commandments, and shall teach men so, he shall be called the least in the kingdom of heaven: but whosoever shall do and teach them, the same shall be called great in the kingdom of heaven. [20]For I say unto you, That except your righteousness shall exceed the righteousness of the scribes and Pharisees, ye shall in no case enter into the kingdom of heaven.**

Why did Jesus say that no one should think He came to destroy the law? To put it another way, what had Jesus done to prompt anyone to make such an accusation? When Stephen was brought before the Sanhedrin, he was accused of trying to "change the customs which Moses delivered" (Acts 6:14). When Paul went to Jerusalem, he was warned that thousands of his countrymen suspected him of teaching his Gentile converts "to forsake Moses" (21:21). Stephen, Paul, and other Christian leaders were accused of a charge first made against Jesus. Throughout His ministry, Jesus often was accused of breaking the Scriptures' ancient commands. The conflict often came when Jesus healed someone on the Sabbath or did something else on that day (Matt. 12:1-14). Jesus was also condemned for ignoring the rules about ritual cleanliness (15:1-2) and for befriending people whom the religious leaders considered unclean (Luke 7:36-50). Matthew 5:17-20 gives His initial answers to those perceptions.

Jesus began by denying that He came **to destroy the law, or the prophets.** To what was He referring? The Hebrew Bible has three categories of books: Law, Prophets, and Writings. Their Books of Law are the same as ours. Their Prophets include our Major and Minor Prophets plus some of what we call History. Their Writings include our Poetry books plus Daniel and some of our books of history. Jesus referred to all three divisions in Luke 24:44, using "the Psalms" to stand for Writings. Sometimes the word *law* referred only to the first five books, the Pentateuch (Luke 2:22). At other times, **law** referred to all the Scriptures (Matt. 5:18). And at still other times **law** was combined with **prophets** to indicate that the reference was to more than the Pentateuch, probably to all the whole Old Testament (v. 17). Thus Jesus was denying that He came to destroy any part of Holy Scripture.

Jesus insisted He came **to fulfill,** not to destroy, the Old Testament. In what ways did Jesus fulfill the Old Testament? First of all, He fulfilled the predictive Scriptures about the nature and mission of the Savior-King. After His resurrection, Jesus opened the minds of the disciples to the many passages that He fulfilled. These passages were from all parts of the Scriptures (Luke 24:44).

Jesus also fulfilled Scripture by interpreting the meaning of the Old Testament. He went behind the letter of the law to its spirit. This is seen in Matthew 5:21-48. And, as the Book of Hebrews points out, Jesus fulfilled the Old Testament by bringing to fruition of some aspects of the Old Testament, such as the end of animal sacrifices.

Verse 18 affirms that the purposes of each part of the Scriptures will be fulfilled. The words **till heaven and earth pass** show that some aspects of the kingdom are still future. Much was fulfilled in Jesus' death and resurrection, but we still pray for His coming kingdom. And the inspired Scriptures continue until the ultimate fulfillment brings us into God's presence forever.

Meanwhile, **one jot or one tittle shall in no wise pass from the law, till all be fulfilled. Jot** stood for "the smallest [Hebrew] letter," and **tittle** stood for "the least stroke of a pen" (NIV). The closest expression in English is to cross the *t* and dot the *i*.

Verses 17-18 show Jesus' relationship to the law. Verses 19-20 focus on followers of Jesus. Verse 19 contains a warning and a challenge. Jesus warned against breaking God's **commandments** or leading someone else to do so. This terminology is used of the Ten Commandments and of God's other laws.

Jesus warned against breaking even the **least commandments.** Since this was so, how much worse is it to break the greater commandments? Jesus said that those who obey and **teach** others to obey the least to the greatest of commandments are considered **great** by God; those who disobey the commandments are unworthy of being considered in **the kingdom.**

The basic lessons of verse 19 are clear. We are to live in light of the Scriptures and to teach others to do the same. And we are to interpret the Old Testament in light of Jesus Christ, who fulfilled it.

Verse 20 was another shocking statement for Jesus' first hearers. **The scribes and Pharisees** were considered by themselves and others to be the best people in the land. Jesus' words would be somewhat like saying "preachers and deacons" to today's hearers. Yet Jesus said that unless the **righteousness** of His disciples surpassed the righteousness of these two groups, they would not be part of God's kingdom. What are the key contrasts between the beliefs and actions of the scribes and Pharisees and the expectations of Jesus for His followers?

We have already noted some of these. Jesus stressed the spirit and divine purpose of the written commandments (vv. 21-42). He called His followers to let others see their good works so people would glorify God and not themselves (v. 16; 6:1). Looking ahead in the Gospel of Matthew we see other examples of the contrast between Jesus and the Pharisees. Jesus is the Son of God who has authority to forgive sins, but the Pharisees called this blasphemy (9:1-8). The Pharisees criticized Jesus for eating with sinners, but Jesus came to seek and save the lost (vv. 10-11). Jesus was moved with compassion on lost people and sent His disciples to help them (v. 36; 10:8).

Matthew 23 is probably the best one source of differences between Jesus and the Pharisees. It consists of a series of woes Jesus pronounced against them. He condemned their pride, which led them to seek to call attention to themselves (23:1-12). He condemned them for religious hypocrisy by claiming to serve God while they were devouring widows' houses, which I assume means taking advantage of the needy (vv. 13-14). Jesus accused them of being zealous to proselytize, but whose goal was to advance their own prestige by gaining new members (v. 15). He accused them of seeking ways to find nonbinding oaths that sounded like authentic promises (vv. 16-22). He said that they emphasized tithing small things but ignored "the more important matters of the law—justice, mercy, and faith" (v. 23, HCSB). This was a key difference. Jesus, probably thinking of Micah 6:8, said that the heart of His way was justice, mercy, and faith—"He hath showed thee, O man, what is good; and what doth the LORD require of thee, but to do justly, and to love mercy, and to walk humbly with thy God?"

What are some lasting truths in Matthew 5:17-20?

1. Because Jesus fulfilled the Old Testament, we should interpret the Bible in light of Him.
2. We should be lifetime students and doers of God's Word.
3. Followers of Jesus follow His ways instead of the legalism of pharisaic types.
4. The righteousness of Jesus' followers is Christ's righteousness, not their own self-righteousness.

❖ *Spiritual Transformations*

Believers should have an impact for Jesus Christ on society. Jesus entrusted to His followers the need to be like salt to sinful people. Christians are to be to the people of the earth what salt is to food—a preservative against corruption. This is a call to be a good influence for the Lord. Jesus also called His disciples to be lights in a sin-darkened world. They are to let their lives shine as lights by letting others see their good works and glorify their Heavenly Father. Jesus came to fulfill the Holy Scriptures. He commands obedience to God's Word. His way, not the way of the scribes and Pharisees, is God's will for all Christians.

*In what ways does your life impact the world for Christ?*________

____

*What will you do to increase your impact for Him?*____________

Prayer of Commitment: Lord, thank You for giving me opportunities to be salt and light. Help me to have the kind of impact that You want from your followers on my society and among my friends. Amen.

[1]Herschel H. Hobbs, *An Exposition of the Gospel of Matthew* [Grand Rapids: Baker Book House, 1965], 63.

Week of October 21

THE HEART OF THE MATTER

Bible Passage: Matthew 5:21-32

❖ *Significance of the Lesson*

• The *Life Question* is, So long as I don't *do* anything wrong, I'm OK, right?

• The *Biblical Truth* is that righteousness is as much a matter of one's heart or attitude as one's actions.

• The *Life Impact* is designed to help you follow Jesus and live according to His teachings by recognizing that sin is in the heart and then determining to deal promptly and decisively with any sin in your life.

Comparative Righteousness

Adults are prone to compare themselves with people whose morality seems worse than theirs. They say: "At least I don't do what ______ does." "I know I'm not perfect, but I do better than ______." "If _____ goes to heaven, I have nothing to worry about." In such cases, they are comparing their actions with the observable actions of others. Theirs is a self-righteousness based on comparison to those whose actions appear to be worse. God judges us not only by our actions but also by our attitudes. And none of us knows another person's attitudes or all that person's actions.

Phrase Study: *Offend Thee*

The Greek verb in Matthew 5:29-30 *skandalizo* is related to the noun *skandalon.* The latter word often referred to a trap or snare or to a stumbling block. The verb thus could apply to something or someone being either a snare or a stumbling block. It can be translated "causes you to sin" (NIV, HCSB). It does not force us to sin, but it lures us toward sin.

❖ *Search the Scriptures*

Jesus expanded the Old Testament prohibition against murder to include the attitude of one's heart and urged His followers to promptly seek reconciliation as soon as they knew of a problem with another person. Jesus also expanded the Old Testament teaching on adultery to cover the attitude of one's heart and urged His followers to diligently guard their hearts against anything that could cause them to sin. And Jesus expanded the Old Testament teaching on divorce to emphasize the impact of one's actions on others.

Know Your Heart (Matt. 5:21-26)

Why is murder *a more precise translation than* ***kill****? What other sins did Jesus condemn? Why did Jesus stress the urgency of reconciliation?*

Verses 21-22: **Ye have heard that it was said by them of old time, Thou shalt not kill; and whosoever shall kill shall be in danger of the judgment: [22]But I say unto you, That whosoever is angry with his brother without a cause shall be in danger of the judgment: and whosoever shall say to his brother, Raca, shall be in danger of the council: but whosoever shall say, Thou fool, shall be in danger of hell fire.**

Jesus began with the Sixth Commandment, **Thou shalt not kill** (Ex. 20:13; Deut. 5:17). Most newer translations use the word "murder" (NIV, HCSB). The Old Testament focused this Commandment on murder. It excluded from this prohibition such things as self-defense, accidental manslaughter, wars that God ordered, and capital punishment when carried out according to due process. The last part of verse 21 was not part of the Sixth Commandment, but it is part of the Mosaic law. According to such passages as Exodus 21:12, murderers are subject to the judgment of the community.

Jesus agreed with the Commandment against the act of murder, but He disagreed with those who restricted the Commandment to the act of murder. What was revolutionary about His teaching in verse 22 was that He challenged everyone to look behind the act of murder to the attitudes and inner sins that can lead to murder. Jesus agreed that murder is a crime that deserves punishment, but He also taught that anger is a sin worthy of **judgment.** Jesus warned that anger against a **brother** is a violation of the spirit of the Sixth Commandment.

Not all anger is sinful. Jesus was angry when He saw those who had turned the temple into a marketplace (Matt. 21:12-17). Righteous indignation, especially on behalf of others, is right. Christians sometimes try to excuse their selfish anger as righteousness anger. "Let us admit it—by and large we are quick to be angry when we are personally affronted and offended, and slow to be angry when sin and injustice multiply in other areas," wrote D. A. Carson.[1]

Jesus also condemned the use of angry and abusive words. Bible students debate the meaning of **Raca.** Most agree that it was a term of abuse that attacked a person's intelligence. Some proposed English translations include "nitwit," "blockhead," "stupid," "moron," "numskull," and "bonehead." The word **fool** is an attack not only on one's intelligence but also on one's religion and character. We have an old saying, "Sticks and stones may break my bones, but words will never hurt me." The Bible disagrees. Proverbs 18:21 says, "Death and life are in the power of the tongue." Loving words give encouragement, hope, and life. Abusive words destroy people's spirits and sometimes life itself. How many children have been the objects of a barrage of angry putdowns? how many husbands and wives? No doubt Jesus had such situations in mind in verse 22.

Jesus condemned anger and abusive language against fellow believers, but He surely didn't justify it anywhere. The place to learn how to practice love and respect for others is in the Heavenly Father's family. Our love is to reflect His love. As Paul wrote, "All bitterness, anger and wrath, insult and slander must be removed from you, along with all wickedness. And be kind and compassionate to one another, forgiving one another, just as God also forgave you in Christ" (Eph. 4:31-32, HCSB).

Jesus mentioned three levels of judgment. **The judgment** may refer to the local court that tried murder cases. **The council** ("Sanhedrin," NIV, HCSB) was the highest Jewish court. **Hell fire** referred to eternal condemnation by God. Jesus was not assigning certain sins to each level of judgment. He was saying that anger and abusive words are not tried in human courts, but they will be judged and punished by God.

Keep in mind this word of caution as you interpret and apply verse 22. Jesus was clearly condemning anger and abusive words as sins. They are the kinds of sins of the heart that sometimes lead to murder. Even when they don't, they are still sins against God, others, and ourselves. Anger and abuse that stop short of murder are sins, but they can be overcome with God's help. No one should say, "Since I am guilty of the sin of anger, I may as well commit murder." Obviously, this was not the conclusion Jesus wanted anyone to draw from His words.

Verses 23-26: **Therefore if thou bring thy gift to the altar, and there rememberest that thy brother hath aught against thee; 24leave there thy gift before the altar, and go thy way; first be reconciled to thy brother, and then come and offer thy gift. 25Agree with thine**

adversary quickly, whiles thou art in the way with him; lest at anytime the adversary deliver thee to the judge, and the judge deliver thee to the officer, and thou be cast into prison. [26]Verily I say unto thee, Thou shalt by no means come out thence, till thou hast paid the uttermost farthing.

Jesus gave two applications of the principle. The first had a religious setting and involved reconciliation with a **brother** (vv. 23-24). The second had a secular setting and involved an **adversary** (vv. 25-26).

Jesus first applied the principle to a disciple in a place of worship. Suddenly you "remember that your brother has something against you" (NIV, HCSB). The Greek word translated **aught** or "something" is a two-letter word. The problem may seem small to the would-be worshiper, but the offended brother doesn't consider it small. An unresolved issue—however small—can grow unto full-scale alienation.

The good news is that a fellowship problem can be solved when there is a spirit of love for each other. Because God has reconciled us to Him, we can seek reconciliation with fellow Christians. Notice that Jesus focused on a situation in which another believer has something against you. In 18:15-17 He dealt with a situation when you feel mistreated by a fellow Christian. In both cases reconciliation is the goal.

To emphasize the urgency of reconciliation, Jesus told us to do it **first**; then return and offer our gifts. We often presume that we have time to repair relationship problems, but for any number of reasons that is not always the case.

Jesus' second application in verses 25-26 deals with a problem regarding an **adversary.** As in verses 23-24, the other person has the grievance—in this case a grievance that could lead to court action. Also as in the first application, Jesus told His disciples to act **quickly.** Jesus' emphases on both an **adversary** and a **brother** show that we have responsibilities for human relationships with all kinds of people.

Jesus was not giving legal advice but stating a principle. He did not tell us what the adversary's accusation was. Verse 26 seems to indicate that it was an unpaid debt. Jesus implied that the adversary might win his case in court, so it was imperative to settle out of court. There was the need to take swift and decisive action.

What are some lasting truths in Matthew 5:21-26?

1. Attitudes as well as actions are subject to divine judgment.
2. Murder is a terrible sin, but so are anger and abusive words.
3. When there is a fellowship problem with a fellow Christian, be quick to seek reconciliation.

4. In relations with unbelievers, seek to live in peace, confessing when you do wrong.

Guard Your Heart (Matt. 5:27-30)

Why is adultery such a serious sin? Why does lust have such a strong hold on human beings? How did Jesus show the urgency and importance of overcoming lust?

Verses 27-30: **Ye have heard that it was said by them of old time, Thou shalt not commit adultery: [28]But I say unto you, That whosoever looketh on a woman to lust after her hath committed adultery with her already in his heart. [29]And if thy right eye offend thee, pluck it out, and cast it from thee: for it is profitable for thee that one of thy members should perish, and not that thy whole body should be cast into hell. [30]And if thy right hand offend thee, cut it off, and cast it from thee: for it is profitable for thee that one of thy members should perish, and not that thy whole body should be cast into hell.**

No area of human conduct has drifted so far from its biblical moorings as our society's attitudes and sexual practices. Christianity came into a world where men were expected to have a mistress or to visit prostitutes. Marriage only provided legitimacy for a man's children. Sexual perversions were common. Society in the Greco-Roman world condoned and often encouraged such things. Christianity impacted and changed this sexual wilderness. For centuries, society gave at least lip service to Christian views of sex and marriage. Then came the sexual revolution of the 1960s that has returned our society to the ancient sexual wilderness.

Matthew 5:27-30 contains some of Jesus' teaching on the subject of sexual morality. He began with the Seventh Commandment, **Thou shalt not commit adultery** (Ex. 20:14; Deut. 5:18). The Commandment was designed to protect marriage and the family. Strictly speaking, the Commandment condemned sexual relations in which at least one of the participants is married to someone other than the person with whom he or she is having sex. But Jesus went behind the letter of the law to its spirit: "But I tell you that anyone who looks at a woman lustfully has already committed adultery with her in his heart" (NIV). Several years ago a prominent person was interviewed about his sexual practices. He strongly affirmed his loyalty to his wife; but being familiar with what Jesus taught about lust, he confessed to sometimes struggling to avoid lust. The public response to this honest confession was blown out of proportion by people with no background in the Bible. Many thought the man's concern to be quaint and old-fashioned. That response showed how far our society had drifted from basic biblical standards.

Jesus' words strongly imply that the Pharisees limited the Commandment to the act of committing adultery. The Seventh Commandment has a tie to the Tenth Commandment, which forbids coveting a neighbor's wife. Many Jews applied this only to the wife of a fellow Jew. They didn't include all sexual lust in their interpretation. Jesus made no such limitation. He used the word **woman** in warning against lust. He warned against being one who **looketh on a woman to lust after her. Looketh** is the present participle of *blepo.* This form of the verb stresses continuous action. Thus the lustful look is not a mere glance but a continuing stare.

The one who gives this stare **hath committed adultery with her already in his heart.** Thus sexual immorality cannot be limited to acts; it can also be committed **in** the **heart.** The Bible does not equate temptation with sin. Everyone is tempted, and everyone sins in some ways. Many people are tempted to lust, but some resist the temptation; others don't. The ones who dwell on lust sometimes follow through with the act. Some may rationalize, "If I'm already a sinner because of my lust, I may as well fulfill my fantasy by committing the act." This is faulty reasoning. Lust alone is a sin, but it does not do the kind of damage that is done by adultery.

John Stott observed: "One wonders if there has ever been a generation in which this teaching of Jesus were more needed or more obviously applicable than our own, in which the river of filth (of pornographic literature and sex films) is in spate. Pornography is offensive to Christians (and indeed to all healthy-minded people) first and foremost because it degrades women from human beings into sex objects, but also because it presents the eye of the beholder with unnatural sexual stimulation. If we have a problem of sexual self-mastery, and if nonetheless our feet take us to these films, and our hands handle this literature, and our eyes feast on the pictures they offer to us, we are not only sinning but actually inviting disaster."[2]

Verses 29-30 show us that Jesus intended for us to control our human thoughts. The **heart** is crux of the problem, but the **eye** and the **hand** often contribute to the adulterous intent of the heart. The word **offend** is often translated "causes you to sin" (NIV, HCSB). The Greek word means to put a stumbling block in front of a person. Jesus did not want anyone to **pluck out** an **eye** or to **cut off** a **hand.** This was

His way of saying that no sacrifice is too great if something is influencing you toward sexual lust. It may be certain books and magazines, movies and TV programs, or computer Web sites or chat rooms.

Some people become addicted to pornography. We know that alcohol, drugs, and gambling can be addictive, but so can pornography. The same steps that are used in treating other addictions are used in helping pornography addicts. Some churches have recovery programs for all of these addictions.

What are some lasting truths in Matthew 5:27-30?

1. Adultery is a serious sin.
2. Lust in the heart is also sinful.
3. Drastic and extreme action is necessary to guard our hearts against sin.
4. Avoiding sin may be costly, but not as costly as giving in to sin.

Consider Your Actions (Matt. 5:31-32)

What were the beliefs of first-century Jews about divorce? What did Jesus teach about marriage and divorce? What Bible verses were involved? What is meant by the words ***saving for the cause of fornication****? How can marriage be such that divorce is rare?*

Verses 31-32: **It hath been said, Whosoever shall put away his wife, let him give her a writing of divorcement: 32But I say unto you, That whosoever shall put away his wife, saving for the cause of fornication, causeth her to commit adultery: and whosoever shall marry her that is divorced committeth adultery.**

Few subjects are so sensitive and potentially controversial as what Jesus taught about marriage and divorce. These teachings are found in Matthew 5:31-32; 19:1-12; Mark 10:1-12; and Luke 16:18. Bible students disagree about the meaning and application of some words and phrases in these teachings.

Matthew 19:1-12 sheds light on major differences between Jesus and the Pharisees. They were preoccupied with discussing the grounds for divorce. He was more interested in the institution of marriage. They debated the meaning and application of Deuteronomy 24:1-4, but Jesus went back to the beginning in Genesis 2:24. God's plan was for marriage to be a lifetime commitment of a man and a woman. The provision in the law was not a command but a concession to the hardness of human hearts. It was an advance in its day, for a bill of divorce at least showed that the woman had been married. Prior to that time some husbands simply threw their wives out. The law forced the husband to have a reason and to give her a bill of divorce.

The law allowed divorce when a husband "found some uncleanness in her" (Deut. 24:1). The Pharisees were divided over what this fault was. One group followed a rabbi named Hillel. He interpreted "some uncleanness" broadly to include almost anything that displeased the husband. Another group followed Rabbi Shammai, who restricted the meaning to sexual immorality. In Matthew 5:31 Jesus quoted what the people had heard about marriage and divorce. This law had been the basis for the Pharisees' lax attitude toward divorce. Apparently in actual practice many of the Pharisees agreed with Hillel. Herschel H. Hobbs wrote: "Quite naturally the position of Shammai was very unpopular among the Jews as it is in our time. The teaching of Hillel was and is quite convenient."[3]

Matthew 5:32 is probably the key teaching of Jesus about divorce. It focuses on the action of the husband who divorces his wife. Such drastic action must be taken only when all else fails. Divorce is always a sign of falling short of God's purpose for marriage. It takes two to have a marriage, but it takes only one to destroy the one-flesh union that should have lasted a lifetime. The context and tone of Jesus' teachings on marriage and divorce should put the fear of God in anyone who causes the breakup of a marriage.

Verse 32 is directed against the husband who divorces his wife, except **for the cause of fornication.** Bible students debate the meaning of **fornication.** This is the Greek word *porneia,* a different word from the word for adultery in verse 27 *(moicheuo).* The word there referred to sexual relations between married people who are not married to each other. This, strictly speaking, defines *adultery. Porneia* is a more general term for all forms of sexual immorality. The term covers adultery, but it also covers prostitution and premarital sexual intercourse. Some Bible students believe Jesus was still thinking only of adultery, but others broaden the application. Some even think that the primary reference was to a husband's discovery that his wife was not a virgin.

What did Jesus say about women who are divorced, even though they were not guilty of any form of sexual immorality? He said that the husband who divorces an innocent wife **causeth her to commit adultery.** How does becoming a divorcee cause an innocent wife to commit adultery? Many Bible students believe that she is tempted to remarry and that if she does both she and the man she marries commit adultery. What about remarrying after a divorce? My understanding is that if a husband divorces his wife to marry someone else, the first wife is free to remarry since her husband has broken the one-flesh union of a married couple. But what if the husband did not break the one-flesh union by his own immorality? Then by divorcing his innocent wife, he causes her and her new husband to commit adultery. In such situations Craig L. Blomberg reminded us, "There is no indication here that a second marriage, even following an illegitimate divorce, is seen as permanently adulterous."[4]

Jesus spoke of the ideal for marriage, but in practice He showed mercy and forgiveness for all sorts of sins, including sexual sins. We remember the woman at the well who had had five husbands and was living with a man (John 4:4-26). Also there was the sinful woman who upset Simon the Pharisee by anointing the feet of Jesus (Luke 7:36-50). And there was the woman taken in adultery (John 8:1-11). When we look at a biblical ideal, we also must not overlook the possibilities of a new start based on the mercy and grace of the Lord.

The divorce rate in our land is appalling. About half of marriages fail. This is true of church people as of others. What can be done? (1) Confront the unmarried with the biblical standard of marriage as more than a conditional contract but as a lifetime commitment. Too many people begin marriage with a kind of tentativeness, thinking they can get out of the relationship if they later choose to do so. (2) Help married people grow in love for each other. More than any other human relationship, marriage requires nurturing and maturing. (3) Practice the kind of love in 1 Corinthians 13. This self-giving love focuses on meeting the needs of the other person. (4) Do everything possible to avoid divorce. Let divorce become an option only if all other options fail. (5) Maintain your mutual faith in God. Tragically, many young couples have no real religious faith. As someone has said, "They need tangible resources, but they need intangible resources even more."

The church must minister to divorced people in the name of Christ. Many divorced people are innocent victims of a tragedy. They don't need rebuking so much as they need love and acceptance in the family of God. The same is true of the children of divorces.

People often say when they sin, "I'm hurting no one but myself." What's wrong with this claim? Our actions always touch the lives of many people. Those who live as salt and light see the good fruit borne by true righteousness. Those who are guilty of one of the sins mentioned in this lesson (murder, anger, abusive words, adultery, lust, and divorce) have a negative impact on others. Some people who initiate a divorce talk as if this will be good for all concerned. They refuse to see the hurt and pain caused by their attitudes and actions. The divorced spouse and the children suffer the most, but the initiator demands what he or she calls "my right to happiness." This is not to say that divorce is never justified. Continual abuse or unfaithfulness sometimes leaves only two options, neither of them good. But divorce is a choice between bad and worse. Human hearts are still hard.

What are some lasting truths in Matthew 5:31-32?

1. The impact of our actions affects us and others.
2. Divorce, for example, hurts everyone involved and devastates some.
3. Christians are to uphold the standard for marriage taught by Jesus.

❖ *Spiritual Transformations*

This lesson deals with three examples of how the righteousness of Christians differs from that of the Pharisees (v. 20). Jesus dealt with murder-anger, adultery-lust, and divorce-influence. He agreed with the Pharisees that the Sixth Commandment condemns murder, but He also condemned anger and abusive words. He challenged His followers to be quick to be reconciled with another Christian. He urged swift action to avoid problems with an adversary. Jesus condemned adultery. But He also condemned the lustful looks that lie in back of sexual immorality. Jesus called in question the divorce law as interpreted by the Pharisees. He taught that marriage is intended to be a lifetime commitment of one man and one woman.

*How did Jesus use the word "heart" in verse 28?*____________

Review the Life Question: "So long as I don't do *anything wrong, I'm OK, right? How would you answer this question?*____________

*What could you do to increase the health of your inner being?*_____

____

Prayer of Commitment: As David said, "Create in me a clean heart, O God; and renew a right spirit within me" (Ps. 51:10). Amen.

[1]D. A. Carson, *The Sermon on the Mount* [Grand Rapids: Baker Book House, 1978], 42.

[2]Stott, *The Message of the Sermon on the Mount*, 90.

[3]Herschel H. Hobbs, *An Exposition of the Gospel of Matthew*, 256.

[4]Craig L. Blomberg, "Matthew," vol. 22 in the New American Commentary [Nashville: Broadman Press, 1992], 111.

Week of October 28

R-E-S-P-E-C-T—FIND OUT WHAT IT MEANS

Bible Passage: Matthew 5:33-48

❖ *Significance of the Lesson*

• The *Life Question* is, How can I demonstrate appropriate respect for those around me?

• The *Biblical Truth* is that Jesus taught believers to practice honesty, exceed the expected, and love their enemies.

• The *Life Impact* is designed to help you follow Jesus and live according to His teachings by comparing your lifestyle with the lifestyle Jesus taught and then assessing how you will more closely follow the lifestyle Jesus taught.

Needed: More Respect for Others

Respect is something everyone needs to receive and to give. Respect is treating another person as a person of value. We are obligated to respect all people, especially older people, parents, and leaders. Actually all people deserve a basic respect—younger people, children, and followers. Insofar as we see others as God sees them, we should respect them. Matthew 5:33-48 focuses on three areas in which respect is expected of us by the Lord. These verses are among the most demanding verses in God's Word. They deal with swearing, retaliation, and love for enemies. Then the chapter ends with a call to be perfect.

An Eye for an Eye

The Jewish law of equal retaliation (sometimes called the *lex talionis* or "measure for measure") was stated this way in Exodus 21:22-25: "When men get in a fight . . . if there is an injury, then you must give life for life, eye for eye, tooth for tooth, hand for hand, foot for foot, burn for burn, bruise for bruise, wound for wound" (HCSB). Prior to this law, people often took vengeance for themselves and often did greater harm than they had received; thus, this was an advance in its day. But Jesus went beyond this ancient law in Matthew 5:38-42. Let's see how.

❖ *Search the Scriptures*

Jesus reminded His disciples that the Old Testament required keeping promises to God. The Pharisees had found ways of getting around that commandment. Jesus said that oaths should not be necessary in daily life because our words should speak only what is true. Jesus reminded them of Old Testament teachings on retaliation—an eye for an eye and a tooth for a tooth. He called for no retaliation and gave four challenging examples of giving back good for evil. Jesus pointed out that they had been taught to love their neighbors and to hate their enemies. He called them to love their enemies. He said that if they loved only friends, they would do no more than pagans did. He also called them to be perfect as their Father in heaven is perfect.

Honesty Is the Best Policy (Matt. 5:33-37)

Why is it important to keep promises made to others, especially those made to God? How were the Pharisees getting around the requirement to keep their promises? What did Jesus say about taking oaths? Does this apply to such things as swearing allegiance to the flag or swearing an oath in court?

Verses 33-37: **Again, ye have heard that it hath been said by them of old time, Thou shalt not forswear thyself, but shalt perform unto the Lord thine oaths: 34But I say unto you, Swear not at all; neither by heaven; for it is God's throne: 35nor by the earth; for it is his footstool: neither by Jerusalem; for it is the city of the great King. 36Neither shalt thou swear by thy head, because thou canst not make one hair white or black. 37But let your communication be, Yea, yea; Nay, nay: for whatsoever is more than these cometh of evil.**

As earlier, Jesus began with what the people had been taught. Verse 33 is not a quotation of a single Old Testament verse. It expressed the gist of what is taught several times in passages, such as Exodus 20:7; Leviticus 19:11-12; Numbers 30:2; and Deuteronomy 23:21-23. These verses warn against making a false statement or promise to God or to others and then not keeping it, especially if the person swore by God's name. Sometimes, then and now, someone will **swear** in order to ensure that he is telling the truth about the past, present, or future. The promises or **oaths** were made in the name of God or something else considered sacred. In essence, this kind of swearing called God to be a witness that the statement was true or the promise would be kept. The Old Testament commandments stressed the evils of false swearing and the need to perform vows.

The Pharisees had developed ways to make statements that were not true and promises that they did not intend to keep. Instead of using the name of God—which if used had to refer to something true—they used some holy-sounding words that they did not consider binding. Verses 34-36 give examples. They apparently swore **by heaven . . . by the earth . . . by Jerusalem . . . by** their **head,** but felt that these high-sounding words were nonbinding since they hadn't actually used God's name. Jesus reminded them that **heaven** is **God's throne,** that God made **the earth,** that **Jerusalem** is God's **city,** and that we cannot change our real **hair.** Jesus spoke about this in greater detail in 23:16-22.

This kind of swearing was like a person making an impressive statement or promise with his fingers crossed behind his back. The one who does this may fool another person, but he doesn't fool God. God knows which statements are true and which promises are kept. Many people make false statements and in crisis times make promises to God that they never keep. No one wins when trying to play word games with God.

This explains Jesus' teaching to **swear not at all.** Rather, Jesus said, **Let your communication be, Yea, yea; Nay, nay** or in other words, "Let your word 'yes' be 'yes,' and your 'no' be 'no'" (HCSB). Jesus' meaning was clear. Since swearing had become so frivolous, it was best not to swear at all. In other words, He taught that our words should be so unquestionably true that an oath is unnecessary, even a distraction. The word **evil** probably refers to "the evil one" (NIV, HCSB), who is a liar, and the father of lies (John 8:44).

Integrity in speech is important. Truth and honesty are essential for ongoing human relationships. The Bible condemns lying in any of its various expressions. One of the things that God hates is "a lying tongue" (Prov. 6:17). In the New Testament believers are instructed, "Lie not one to another" (Col. 3:9).

"Two questions may arise in our minds at this point. First, if swearing is forbidden, why has God Himself used oaths in Scripture? Why, for example, did He say to Abraham: 'By myself I have sworn . . .

I will indeed bless you . . .'? To this I think we must answer that the purpose of the divine oaths was not to increase His credibility (since 'God is not man that He should lie'), but to elict and confirm our faith. The fault which made God condescend to this human level lay not in any untrustworthiness of His but in our unbelief.

"Secondly, if swearing is forbidden, is the prohibition absolute? For example, should Christians, in order to be consistent in their obedience, decline to . . . give evidence on oath in a court of law? The Anabaptists took this line in the sixteenth century and most Quakers still do today. While admiring their desire not to compromise, one can still perhaps question whether their interpretation is not excessively literalistic. After all, Jesus Himself, Matthew later records, did not refuse to reply when the high priest put Him on oath, saying, 'I adjure you by the living God, tell us if you are the Christ, the Son of God.' He confessed that He was and that later they would see Him enthroned at God's right hand. What Jesus emphasized in His teaching was that honest men do not need to resort to oaths; it was not that they should refuse to take an oath if required by some external authority to do so."[1]

What are some lasting truths in Matthew 5:33-37?

1. We demonstrate respect for God, others, and ourselves when we practice straightforward honesty.
2. That which is not honest is from the Devil, the father of lies.
3. Having to use oaths to convince people we are telling the truth should convince us that we have not made honesty our policy.

Beyond the Call of Duty (Matt. 5:38-42)

*Why was the law of equal retribution an advance in its day? What does the word **evil** mean in verse 39? What four examples of His teaching on retaliation did Jesus give? Why are these teachings of Jesus challenging to put into practice?*

Verses 38-42: **Ye have heard that it hath been said, An eye for an eye, and a tooth for a tooth: 39But I say unto you, That ye resist not evil: but whosoever shall smite thee on thy right cheek, turn to him the other also. 40And if any man will sue thee at the law, and take away thy coat, let him have thy cloak also. 41And whosoever shall compel thee to go a mile, go with him twain. 42Give to him that asketh thee, and from him that would borrow of thee turn not thou away.**

Jesus was listing ways in which His righteousness is superior to that of the Pharisees (5:20). Verses 38-42 deal with the differences in their teachings about retaliation. The people were familiar with the Old Testament teaching of limited retaliation—**an eye for an eye, and a tooth for a tooth.** This law came straight out of the Mosaic law's civil code, which was designed to provide justice (Ex. 21:24; Lev. 24:19-20; Deut. 19:21). The intention of the law was to restrain individual revenge by restricting the degree of punishment. Prior to this time, a vengeful person might kill someone who knocked out his tooth. Or someone blinded in one eye might put out both eyes of the perpetrator. Apparently the Pharisees quoted this law to justify taking personal vengeance.

Rather than retaliation and revenge, Jesus stated His way in verse 39, saying, **Resist not evil.** The word for **evil** can be either neuter (a thing) or masculine (a being). Thus it can mean "evil" or "an evil being." The same word appeared in verse 37, where most modern translations have "the evil one," meaning the Devil. But it cannot refer to the Devil in verse 39 because Jesus said not to resist the being and James said to resist the Devil (Jas. 4:7). Thus Jesus was probably referring to an evil person, hence the *New International Version*'s "an evil person" and the *Holman Christian Standard Bible*'s "an evildoer." Jesus had in mind someone who does evil against you. The *Good News Bible* catches Jesus' meaning well: "Do not take revenge on someone who wrongs you" (GNB).

Jesus did not mean that evil people never should be resisted. God ordained governments to protect society against evildoers. Thus in verses 39b-42 Jesus gave four situations from first-century Jewish life to illustrate what He meant. These illustrations show how Jesus sought not only to restrain personal revenge but also to replace it with His kind of love. An evil person gives back evil for good. A natural response is to give back evil for evil. But Jesus taught His followers to give back good for evil.

Jesus' first illustration involves responding to a personal insult. Being struck on the **right cheek** by a right-handed person meant a backhanded slap. This was more an insult than an injury. Jesus was showing His disciples how to respond to a backhanded blow and any kind of personal insult. When we are insulted, we are tempted to respond in kind. But Jesus said to **turn to him the other** [cheek] **also.** Rather than hurling an insult back, absorb the insult and continue to be vulnerable to insults against yourself. Jesus is the perfect example of how to practice this response. All sorts of abuse and insults were hurled at Him, yet He did not strike back. By contrast, many people trade insult for insult and blow for blow. This only fuels the fires of hatred and conflict.

The second illustration of Jesus' teaching on nonretaliation is even more difficult than the first. It concerns responding to someone who chooses to **sue** you for some possession. In Jesus' day a poor person had two articles of clothing—a **coat** ("tunic," NIV) and a **cloak.** The tunic was a long garment with sleeves that was worn next to the body. The other garment was a cloak worn over the tunic. This was an all-purpose garment for poor people. It was often the only blanket a poor person had. The Old Testament proclaimed special protection for a person's cloak. If it was taken as a pledge for a debt, it had to be returned by sundown (Ex. 22:26-27; Deut. 24:12-13). A widow's cloak was never be taken as a pledge of a debt (v. 17).

Jesus set up a situation in which an evil person was threatening to sue a disciple for his tunic. Jesus added, **Let him have thy cloak also.** The person was not asking for the cloak, only the tunic; but Jesus said to volunteer to throw in the cloak as well. Remember, Jesus was not referring to an optional overcoat but to an essential garment. A person without a tunic and cloak would be without any clothes.

Jesus' third illustration comes from a well-known ancient practice. The word **compel** ("forces," NIV, HCSB) translates the Greek word *angareuo,* which goes back to a Persian custom. The *angaroi* were couriers placed along the road at fixed locations. They had the power to conscript travelers to do errands for the king. So the verb can signify forced labor. The same word is used of the Roman soldier who forced Simon to carry Jesus' cross (Matt. 27:32; Mark 15:21). A Roman soldier could demand that a Jew carry his equipment for **a mile.** The law did not allow the soldier to force the Jew to carry it more than a mile. This was a classic example of the kind of exploitation throughout history by people with power to force others to do their bidding.

The Romans had conquered the land of the Jews, so most of the Jews hated the Romans. When a member of the Roman occupation forces compelled a Jew to carry his baggage, most Jews seethed with a desire to get even. Jesus taught His followers that when they were forced to carry a soldier's pack for a mile, they should volunteer to carry it for another mile. Imagine the discipline and love needed for a Jewish believer to absorb the humiliation and exploitation and go the second mile. And all of this needed to be done in good spirits, not reluctantly.

We need to remind ourselves that Jesus was not condoning exploitation. He was speaking of the human temptation to want to get even for hurt inflicted on us personally.

Imagine how a Roman soldier would have responded if a Jew did what Jesus taught and cheerfully carried his burden one mile then gladly took it another mile. That would attract attention and perhaps open the door of someone's heart. So when we speak of "going the second mile," we are talking about going beyond what is required and expected.

Jesus' fourth illustration seems almost anticlimactic after looking at examples of people who insult you, sue you for all you have, and exploit you with heavy and unfair demands. However, His fourth illustration is one that happens often in our lives. It is of someone asking you for money—either a gift or a loan. Jesus may have had two people in mind—one who asks for a gift and another who asks for a loan. Or He may have had one person in mind who asks for both. As we know, many loans end up becoming gifts.

Most of us have mixed feelings about people who ask for a gift or who are slow to repay loans. We are to help people in need, but we resent being conned by a clever lie. Bible students often try to figure out whether Jesus intent related to all requests or to only real needs. Jesus seems to have used an extreme example to emphasize the need for generous giving to others.

Jesus expects us to give to others, but He also expects us to be faithful stewards of what He has given us. We live in a world of unlimited needs, yet each of us has limited resources. We must learn to use our limited needs to meet the greatest needs. Jesus did not say to give whatever you are asked but to give to whomever asks.

What are some lasting truths in Matthew 5:38-42?

1. Christians are not to retaliate against those who harm them; instead, they are to show love.
2. Christians are not to trade insults.
3. Christians are not to insist on their own rights.
4. Christians are to do more than is expected of them.
5. Christians are to be generous.

Love Your Enemies (Matt. 5:43-48)

*Where had Jesus' hearers heard that they should hate their enemies? What groups should we love? How can we love our enemies? What is the source of love? In what sense are we to **be . . . perfect**?*

Verses 43-48: **Ye have heard that it hath been said, Thou shalt love thy neighbor, and hate thine enemy. 44But I say unto you, Love your enemies, bless them that curse you, do good to them that hate you, and pray for them which despitefully use you, and persecute you; 45that ye may be the children of your Father which is in heaven: for he maketh his sun to rise on the evil and on the good, and sendeth rain on the just and on the unjust. 46For if ye love them which love you, what reward have ye? do not even the publicans the same? 47And if ye salute your brethren only, what do ye more than others? do not even the publicans so? 48Be ye therefore perfect, even as your Father which is in heaven is perfect.**

Jesus said that His disciples had **heard** to **love** their **neighbor** but to **hate** their **enemy.** The Old Testament clearly commanded, **Love thy neighbor** (Lev. 19:18), but it does not say, **hate thine enemy.** In fact, passages such as Exodus 23:4 commanded the Israelites to help their enemies. Proverbs 25:21 says, "If thine enemy be hungry, give him bread to eat; and if he be thirsty, give him water to drink." What then was the source of the teaching to hate their enemies? John Broadus wrote: "The Jewish teachers held that an enemy was not a neighbor, and that the command to love the latter implied permission to withhold it from the former."[2]

People who hated their enemies were trying to justify their own evil practices. They defined neighbors as people of their own kind and excluded people who were different. The Jews could exclude Gentiles, which included the hated Romans. The Pharisees could exclude tax collectors and sinners from their own group. This tendency to restrict the definition of **neighbor** is seen in the question to Jesus, "Who is my neighbor?" (Luke 10:29). Jesus told a parable to show that no one can be excluded from a person's love (vv. 30-37). And here in Matthew 5:43-47 He made clear that His definition of **neighbor** included one's **enemy.**

Verse 44 clearly records Jesus' teaching to **love your enemies.** This demand sounds difficult, if not impossible. How can you love people who **curse you . . . hate you . . . despitefully use you, and persecute you**? This brings us face to face with the nature of Christian love. Love for enemies is not a warm, fuzzy feeling of affection. Christian love is an action, not an emotion or a feeling. Christ's love is something you do. Verse 44, along with the parallel passage in Luke 6:27-28, list specific actions that constitute Christian love for enemies. Christians are to **bless them . . . do good to them . . . and pray for them.**

By the very definition, enemies are people whom we don't like and who don't like us. They do hurtful things to us. If we wait until we have warm feelings for them, we probably will never show love for them. If you would love them, act for their good—however you may feel. Often positive actions eventually produce better feelings.

Love in English can have many meanings, but the Greek language had different words for erotic love, family love, brotherly love, and God's kind of love. His *agape* love is the basis for our salvation and the pattern for our living. It is a self-giving love that acts for the good of the ones who are loved. This kind of love is the kind shown by **the children of your Father which is in heaven.** His love is full and rich toward all people. He sends the sunshine and the rain on all people—good or bad (Matt. 5:45)—and He desires to give to all people His greatest gift—salvation (2 Pet. 3:9).

In Matthew 5:46-47 Jesus called His followers to live by His kind of love. Most people love people who love them. They easily do good for those who do good for them. Only an abnormal person fails to respond to love from friends. Even pagans show that kind of love. Christians love other believers, but we also are called to love and do good for those who are not our friends.

Verse 48 is an appropriate conclusion not only to verses 43-48 but to verses 21-48 as well. The word rendered **perfect** is *teleios*, which means "be mature" or "be perfect." We know that no one but Jesus ever was sinlessly perfect, but that still remains our goal. We believe that someday we will be like Him, and we are growing in His image in the present world. Paul expressed the Christian idea of perfection when he wrote: "Not as though I had already attained, either were already perfect: but I follow after, if that I may apprehend that for which also I am apprehended of Christ Jesus. Brethren, I count not myself to have apprehended: but this one thing I do, forgetting those things which are behind, and reaching forth for those things which are before, I press toward the mark for the prize of the high calling of God in Christ Jesus" (Phil. 3:12-14). God's ultimate goal for His children is nothing less than perfection. A mother would not tell her children to be 90 percent honest or even 99 percent honest. She would tell her children to be honest all the time. When they fall short, she doesn't throw them out. She helps them grow toward the goal. So does our Heavenly Father expect nothing less than the best from His children, and when we fail, He forgives us and helps us to move on toward the goal.

What are some lasting lessons in Matthew 5:43-48?

1. People tend to love only their friends, but Jesus calls His followers to love all people—brothers, neighbors, and even enemies.

2. Christian love is something we do, not merely a feeling.

3. Loving only those who love us is nothing different or more than unbelievers do.

4. God calls His people to have the kind of maturity that grows toward ultimate perfection beyond this life.

❖ *Spiritual Transformations*

As Christians, we are to be totally honest in words and deeds. We are to go beyond what people expect by loving them in trying situations. This calls for loving not only our fellow Christians and neighbors but also our enemies. God's goal that we be perfect should be our goal.

What does this lesson teach about the kind of life Jesus wants you to live? ______________________________

In what area do you most need to be transformed? ____________
____

Prayer of Commitment: Lord, help me become increasingly the person You want me to be. Amen.

[1]Stott, *The Message of the Sermon on the Mount,* 101-102.

[2]John A. Broadus, *Commentary on the Gospel of Matthew,* in An American Commentary on the New Testament [Philadelphia: The American Baptist Publication Society, 1886], 121.

Study Theme

Believer's Handbook 201

This is the second part of a two-month study of Jesus' Sermon on the Mount. In the introduction to October's lessons we noted that the Sermon called for a "Christian counter-culture." Jesus' teachings are in contrast to secular society and to the kind of religion that was practiced by the scribes and Pharisees. This is as true of Matthew 6–7 as it is of Matthew 5.

The first lesson in this Study Theme, "Seeking Your Father's Approval," is based on Matthew 6:1-18. Jesus contrasted His motivation for religious acts with that of the Pharisees and with those of pagans. Jesus dealt with motives for giving, praying, and fasting. As Jesus' followers, we should always do the right things and strive to have pure motives.

The second lesson, "The Cure for Anxious Care," is based on Matthew 6:19-34. Jesus contrasted His way of dealing with possessions with the way of the Jews and the ways of the Gentiles. He warned against worshiping things and worrying about things. As Jesus' followers, we should seek first God's kingdom and trust Him to supply our needs.

The third lesson, "20/20 Vision," is based on Matthew 7:1-12. Jesus contrasted His teaching about relationships with the way people often fail in their relationships with others and with God. He warned against harsh judgment and called for careful evaluation based on fruit. The so-called Golden Rule is in this lesson.

The fourth lesson, "Make Up Your Minds," is based on Matthew 7:13-29. This is the **Evangelism Lesson** for this quarter. It contrasts the choices and practices of the world with the choices and practices of Jesus. It includes an invitation to enter the narrow gate to salvation and to walk the hard road of Christian discipleship. Jesus warned about false prophets and about those who presumed on their profession of faith. He closed His Sermon with an emphasis on not only hearing but also obeying God's Word.

Week of November 4

SEEKING YOUR FATHER'S APPROVAL

Bible Passage: Matthew 6:1-18

❖ *Significance of the Lesson*

• The *Life Question* is, Do I follow Jesus for the right reason?

• The *Biblical Truth* is that for followers of Jesus, the Father's approval of their actions should be most important.

• The *Life Impact* is designed to help you live as a follower of Jesus by evaluating your motives for religious practices and then deciding to make paramount the Father's approval of these practices.

The Importance of Motives

Doing the right thing is always important, but doing the right thing for the right reasons is also important. People sometimes do the right thing, but they do it for the wrong reasons. Many adults perform religious practices to be recognized and praised by others. God's approval should be the primary motivation for doing religious practices. Human motivation is seldom completely pure; often we have mixed motives. We should confess our mixed motives and ask God to help us have purer motives; however, we should not stop doing the right things when our motives are not totally pure. For example, we need to participate in public worship on a regular basis. Doing this involves commitment and discipline. On some Sundays you may be highly motivated by gratitude and love, but at other times you may go only out of a sense of duty to your commitment to do the will of God. When our motives are mixed, we should do what God approves, regardless of our feelings at the time; and if our motives are mixed, we should ask God to make them pure.

Word Study: *Vain Repetitions*

The Greek word *battalogeo* in Matthew 6:7 is often translated "babble" or "babbling" (HCSB, NIV). The word describes what pagans called prayer. They had many gods and they believed they should pray to each of their gods. They also believed that the more often a prayer was said, the more likely it was to be answered.

❖ *Search the Scriptures*

Don't do religious practices to receive human praise, but do these acts to please God. Three areas of religious practices are giving, prayer, and fasting. Giving to the poor for personal honor or gain does not receive the Father's approval. Praying to be praised by others receives no reward other than human praise. Prayer is directed to the Father, and Jesus gave the Model Prayer to guide believers. Fasting as a spiritual discipline is not an occasion for self-display but for self-denial.

Giving (Matt. 6:1-4)

*What are **alms**? What is the significance of the word **when** in verse 2? In what sense did some people **sound a trumpet** when they gave alms? What **reward** is mentioned in verse 2? How literally are we to take verse 3?*

Verses 1-4: **Take heed that ye do not your alms before men, to be seen of them: otherwise ye have no reward of your Father which is in heaven. [2]Therefore when thou doest thine alms, do not sound a trumpet before thee, as the hypocrites do in the synagogues and in the streets, that they may have glory of men. Verily I say unto you, They have their reward. [3]But when thou doest alms, let not thy left hand know what thy right hand doeth: [4]that thine alms may be in secret: and thy Father which seeth in secret himself shall reward thee openly.**

"Acts of righteousness" (NIV) is the theme that binds Matthew 6:1-18 to Matthew 5. The "righteousness" of chapter 5 is the moral character of people who know the Lord. It was seen in the Beatitudes (see v. 6) and in Jesus' high standards of righteousness that surpassed "the righteousness of the scribes and Pharisees" (v. 20). The righteousness of 6:1-18 focuses on religious practices—specifically three: giving, praying, and fasting.

These three religious activities or disciplines were part of the life of first-century Jews. Jesus used the word **when,** not "if," in verses 2,5,16 because He assumed that religious people would give, pray, and fast. In 6:1-18 He focused on their motives for doing these acts of religious devotion. One's motives should be to please God, not to receive the praise of other people, but they made a display of their devotion **to be seen of them.**

Alms were gifts given primarily to help the poor, but the principle applies to all giving. The thrust of verses 2-4 is that we should not give be seen and praised but to receive God's approval. God is kind and merciful, and Jesus expects His people to be kind and merciful and to give generously to help the needy. Jesus' words in verses 2-4, however, show that generosity is not enough. The reason we give is important.

Jesus warned against giving like **the hypocrites.** This word originally referred to actors who played a part. In religion, the word refers to people who pretend to be something they are not. People who give in order to be seen are playing the part of a generous giver with a pure heart toward God, when actually they give in such ways as to draw attention and praise to themselves from other people.

Jesus told His followers **not** to **sound a trumpet** when they gave **in the synagogues and in the streets.** We do not know whether anyone ever actually blew a trumpet to call attention to his giving. Possibility Jesus was referring to the noise of money being cast into collection receptacles. More likely, Jesus was describing how some people "blow their own horns" to call attention to their giving. Thus He pictured a pompous Pharisee marching behind trumpeters who were blowing a fanfare calling attention to the person making the gift.

Jesus said, **They have their reward.** They gave in order to receive **glory** from people. Human praise was what they sought; human praise was what they got—and no more. The word **have** translates a Greek verb that commonly was used in business transactions to describe receipt in full, hence the *New International Version*'s "they have received their reward in full." They will not receive a reward from God. To the contrary, those who give **in secret** God will **reward.**

We need to understand verse 3 in light of Jesus' emphasis on secrecy in verse 4. If we had only these two verses on giving, we might conclude that we should make our giving so secret that we ourselves don't know what we give. What did Jesus mean by **let not thy left hand know what thy right hand doeth**? Jesus' point was that not only should we not give with others as an audience but we also should not give with ourselves as the audience. We can take such pride in what we give that the glory does not go to God.

Some people are offended by associating God with giving rewards. These rewards are not merit rewards that earn salvation by good works. They are fruits of a person with a right relationship to God who acts to meet human needs for the glory of God. Some of these rewards are the joy of seeing the needy helped and the satisfaction of receiving God's approval.

What are some lasting truths in Matthew 6:1-4?

1. Religious practices should be done for the glory of God, not for our own glory.

2. People who give in order to be praised have already received their full reward.

3. Giving presents subtle temptations to pride.

Praying (Matt. 6:5-15)

Did Jesus intend for His teaching to be applied to praying in public? What are the similarities between verses 5-8 and verses 2-4? What are the differences? How does what Jesus taught about prayer differ from the ways pagans conduct their prayers? If God already knows our needs, why do we need to pray? Why is "the Model Prayer" a good title for the prayer in verses 9-13? What are the components of the Model Prayer? What do verses 14-15 teach about forgiveness?

Verses 5-8: **And when thou prayest, thou shalt not be as the hypocrites are: for they love to pray standing in the synagogues and in the corners of the streets, that they may be seen of men. Verily I say unto you, They have their reward. 6But thou, when thou prayest, enter into thy closet, and when thou hast shut thy door, pray to thy Father which is in secret; and thy Father which seeth in secret shall reward thee openly. 7But when ye pray, use not vain repetitions, as the heathen do: for they think that they shall be heard for their much speaking. 8Be not ye therefore like unto them: for your Father knoweth what things ye have need of, before ye ask him.**

Jesus repeated some of the same things He said about giving in verses 2-4. He addressed those who act as **hypocrites,** who pray in order to receive human praise. Just as He warned about giving publicly, so He warned about praying **that they may be seen of men.** The public settings of both actions were the same—**standing in the synagogues and in the corners of the streets.** Jesus said of both groups, **They have their reward.**

Jesus was not condemning **standing** when praying or public prayers in general. Both were legitimate ways of praying. Standing is one of several postures in prayer that is commended in the Bible. Standing while praying and public praying are right when the audience is the

Lord, not other people. Following Jesus' instructions rules out praying in order to impress others. He also ruled out being overly impressed about our own praying. A person can take such pride in his praying that he becomes an audience of one. A **shut . . . door** to a private place helps focus our prayer on God. I don't know what the **closet** is to which you go to pray, but each of us needs such a private place.

Jesus had been speaking to Jews about their praying. In verse 7 He warned against the way pagans prayed. He said not to use **vain repetitions** ["don't babble," HCSB], **as the heathen do.** The problem with their prayers was that they thought that repeating the words over and over again made the prayers more likely to be answered favorably. They relied on "their many words" (NIV, HCSB). Jesus was not speaking against persistence in prayer. Jesus Himself persevered in prayer (26:44; Luke 6:12), and He taught His disciples to keep on praying (Matt. 7:7-8; Luke 11:5-13; 18:1-8).

We do not need to overwhelm God with many words. He loves us, and He **knoweth what things ye have need of, before ye ask him.** This fact raises some basic questions: If God knows what we need, why doesn't He simply give us what we need? Why do we need to pray?

Part of the answer is that God gives us many things apart from our prayers. The blessings of His common grace—such as the sunshine and the rain—are examples of such good things (Matt. 5:45). God's best gifts, however, depend on our relationship with Him. God yearns to give us the best gifts, but first we must respond with prayer and obedience.

Verses 9-13: **After this manner therefore pray ye: Our Father which art in heaven, Hallowed be thy name. 10 Thy kingdom come. Thy will be done in earth, as it is in heaven. 11 Give us this day our daily bread. 12 And forgive us our debts, as we forgive our debtors. 13 And lead us not into temptation, but deliver us from evil: For thine is the kingdom, and the power, and the glory, forever. Amen.**

Verse 9-13 usually are called "the Lord's Prayer," but many prefer the term "the Model Prayer." This is not a prayer Jesus prayed, for He never had sins to confess. He gave it to help His followers know how to pray. Sometimes we pray it as it is; at other times we use it to see what areas a prayer should contain. The prayer has two main parts. The first part in verses 9-10 includes three petitions that focus on God—His name, His kingdom, and His will. The second part focuses on three petitions about human needs—daily bread, forgiveness, and deliverance from temptation.

The petitions are addressed to **our Father which art in heaven.** The basic difference between Christian prayer and the prayers of hypocrites and pagans is the God to whom we pray. The title shows our personal relationship to the great and good God. The first petition is that God's **name** be **hallowed.** The prayer is that God's name be set apart for the glory due Him. God's **name** refers to His person and character. Notice that the prayer is addressed to God to bring this to pass.

The same pattern is in the second petition. God is asked to bring in His **kingdom.** This petition, like the other two, does not ask God to help us do these things; only God can bring in His kingdom. People can be used in serving the King, but only God can cause the kingdom to reach its culmination. **Kingdom** refers to God's reign or rule. In one sense the kingdom came in Jesus (Mark 1:15), yet it has to come in all its fullness.

The third petition about God is **thy will be done in earth, as it is in heaven.** This request reinforces the other two. With God's will, as with His name and with His kingdom, the place to begin is to commit these petitions to God, who alone can bring them to pass. Heaven is where God's will is already done perfectly. His will is not being done perfectly on earth. Jesus taught us to pray that His will would triumph on earth.

The first three petitions focus on God and His glory. People who pray like this are out of step with hypocrites who pray to be seen and with the heathen who seek to impress their gods with many words. These petitions are also in stark contrast to the goals of most people. Many want to see their names in lights, not to see God's name glorified. Most are more concerned about their own petty kingdoms than they are about God's kingdom. They strive to impose their own will rather than yearn to see God's will done.

The second set of petitions deals with basic human needs and our dependence on God to meet those needs. The petition in verse 11 acknowledges this and our dependence on God for **bread.** The Greek word rendered **daily** has three possible meanings: (1) for the present day, (2) for tomorrow, or (3) for subsistence. Little practical difference exists between the first two. Used in the morning, it means for today. Used in the evening, it means bread for tomorrow.

Give is followed by **forgive. Debts** is one way to describe sins. These are called **trespasses** ("wrongdoing," HCSB; "sins," NIV) in verses 14 and 15. Sins are debts in the sense of obligations we owe God. The word **debts** stand for everything that we should be and do toward God, others, and ourselves. Until these debts are forgiven, they mar our relationships with God and others. Thus we ask God to **forgive us our debts,** which means to cancel the debts and remove them as barriers to fellowship with Him.

The third petition for us has two parts, both of which present challenges for Bible students. **Lead us not into temptation** sounds as if it is a request that God not tempt us. James 1:13 says that "God is not tempted by evil, and He Himself doesn't tempt anyone" (HCSB). God allows us to be tested, but He does not tempt us. Temptations to do evil come from the Devil and from within us.

In the phrase **deliver us from evil,** the word **evil** can be either neuter or masculine, meaning that it can refer to evil in general or to "the evil one" (NIV, HCSB). Here it probably refers to Satan. Thus verse 13 is a prayer for deliverance from temptations and from Satan's grasp.

Verses 14-15: **For if ye forgive men their trespasses, your heavenly Father will also forgive you: [15]But if ye forgive not men their trespasses, neither will your Father forgive your trespasses.**

Verses 14-15 are not actually part of the prayer, but these words of Jesus help explain the words **as we forgive our debtors** in verse 12b. The prayer for our forgiveness needs to be linked together with a forgiving spirit toward others. Jesus constantly taught that God's forgiving us is inseparable from us forgiving those who sin against us (see 5:7; 18:21-35). God has forgiven us an enormous, unpayable debt. Because of this, He expects us to forgive others who sin against us.

These verses are open to the misunderstanding that forgiving others is a good work that merits God forgiving us. This is not the point. Jesus was saying that people who open their hearts to receive God's forgiveness open their hearts to extend forgiveness to others. The door for forgiveness is either open or closed. If it is open to receive God's forgiveness, it is also open for forgiveness to go out to others. If it is closed to either one, it is closed to both. If it is open, it is open to both.

What are some lasting truths in Matthew 6:5-15?

1. Prayer should be as inconspicuous as possible.
2. Public prayer is appropriate when practiced with right motives.
3. God wants us to give us good gifts, and so He encourages us to keep praying.
4. God knows our needs and gives us many blessings, but our deepest needs are met only as we pray.
5. Our prayer should include all the elements of the Model Prayer.

Fasting (Matt. 6:16-18)

What is the purpose of fasting? What warnings did Jesus give about the wrong way of fasting? What instructions did He give about how to fast?

Verses 16-18: **Moreover when ye fast, be not as the hypocrites, of a sad countenance: for they disfigure their faces, that they may appear unto men to fast. Verily I say unto you, They have their reward.
17But thou, when thou fastest, anoint thine head, and wash thy face;
18that thou appear not unto men to fast, but unto thy Father which is in secret: and thy Father, which seeth in secret, shall reward thee openly.**

Jewish fasting included public fasting, but it was usually a matter of private devotion. It was a way of humbling oneself before God, often in penitence for sin. Fasting and prayer often went together as a person or group sought God's strength and direction. Fasting was also one way of providing food for the hungry.

What about Christian fasting? Jesus said, **When ye fast,** not *if* you fast. Just as He expected His followers to give and pray, so He expected them to fast. Jesus' disciples did not fast the way the disciples of John the Baptist did, but He predicted a time when they would fast (9:14-15). The Pharisees fasted twice a week and made sure others knew about it (Luke 18:12). As He had with giving and praying, Jesus condemned **the hypocrites** who fasted to be praised by men. As with the people who gave and who prayed to be seen, the ones who fast to be seen already have received **their reward** in full.

The hypocrites . . . disfigure their faces so people would know they had been fasting. They tried to look somber. Sometimes they wore sackcloth and poured ashes on their faces. They did whatever they could to be sure that observers would know they had been fasting. Jesus told His disciples to **wash** their **face** and **anoint** their **head** with oil. This was what they did on a normal day. The opposite of this was to **appear** with uncombed hair and eyes red from weeping.

In secret is a theme in Matthew 6:1-18. The Father knows what we do in secret and in public. Jesus wasn't ruling out giving, praying, and fasting. He was warning that religious people are tempted to parade their piety before an audience that will praise them for their acts of devotion.

What are some lasting lessons in Matthew 6:16-18?

1. Believers should not display their seasons of fasting by visible signs of deprivation and suffering.

2. Fasting and prayer go together.

3. When people do some act of sacrifice and devotion, they are often tempted to do or say something to others in hopes of recognition. We must resist this temptation.

❖ *Spiritual Transformations*

As followers of Jesus, we are to do acts of righteousness, such as giving, praying, and fasting. When we do these things, we need to examine our motives. Hypocrites do them to be seen and praised by other people. Such human praise is the only reward these people will ever receive. The goal of religious actions is for us to do them in such ways as to praise God. There are private and public expressions for giving, praying, and fasting; but our basic practice should be that they are done in secret between a believer and God. Public expressions should glorify the Father, not the disciple. In the Model Prayer, Jesus taught believers how to pray and what to pray for.

As you evaluate your motives for giving, praying, and fasting, to what degree do you seek human praise? ____________________

____

Are your motives for your religious practices ever anything other than to please God? ____________________________________

____

How do you deal with the reality of mixed motives? ____________

____

Prayer of Commitment: Lord, help me to do the right things and for the right reasons. Be patient when my motives are mixed. Help me do what is right whatever my motives, and help me increasingly do right to honor You. Amen.

Week of November 11

THE CURE FOR ANXIOUS CARE

Bible Passage: Matthew 6:19-34

❖ *Significance of the Lesson*

- How can I overcome anxieties about life's necessities?
- The *Biblical Truth* is that followers of Jesus love God and trust their Heavenly Father's care to provide basic necessities.
- The *Life Impact* is designed to help you live as a follower of Jesus by acknowledging that substituting materialism for God does not keep anxiety at bay and then determining to trust God for all necessities.

Worrying About Life's Necessities

Many adults worry about life, money, family, and so on. They try to convince themselves that security is found in a good job, in hard work, and in a savings account. Yet they remain anxious about their future. They believe that if they don't worry about these things, no one else will. They feel the pressure of securing the future. In the Sermon on the Mount Jesus had a lot to say about anxiety concerning provisions for the unknown future.

Phrase Study: *Lay up for yourselves treasures in heaven*

Jesus' admonition to **lay up for yourselves treasures in heaven** in Matthew 6:20 is the opposite of laying up treasures on earth. Earthly treasures are easily destroyed. When we die, we leave them all behind. Heavenly treasures are what we take with us to heaven. Although earthly things are held for only a short time, they can be used for eternal ventures. We will leave money, houses, and lands behind, but we will carry with us the person we have become by God's grace, and we will find all those whom God has touched through our witness and ministry.

❖ *Search the Scriptures*

Jesus taught His followers to love God with undivided loyalty. They should lay up treasures in heaven, choose to worship God rather than money, and have single-hearted devotion to God. He warned them against anxiety concerning their material necessities. Such anxiety is useless, dangerous, and pagan. Jesus called believers to seek God above all things and promised to meet the needs of those who do.

The three points in the lesson outline answer the Life Question.

Love God Above All (Matt. 6:19-24)

Why does financial security not exist? What is the main point of verses 22-23? Why can no one ***serve two masters****?*

Verses 19-21: **Lay not up for yourselves treasures upon earth, where moth and rust doth corrupt, and where thieves break through and steal: [20]But lay up for yourselves treasures in heaven, where neither moth nor rust doth corrupt, and where thieves do not break through nor steal: [21]For where your treasure is, there will your heart be also.**

Notice three things that Jesus did not mean in this saying. First, He wasn't placing a ban on owning property. In fact, we have nothing to give unless we have something of our own (Eph. 4:28). Second, Jesus was not condemning planning for the future. The Bible urges us to draw a lesson from the ant that works and stores up provisions (Prov. 6:6-8). Third, Jesus was not calling for an approach to life that rejects the good things of life that God gives us to enjoy.

What then did Jesus mean by His teaching in verses 19-21? The key words in verse 19 are **for yourselves** and **upon earth.** The words **for yourselves** refer to selfish actions. The words **upon earth** refer to earthly things. Jesus warned against selfishly grasping and holding onto material things for yourself. He explained why this was risky. Earthly treasures are in danger because they are subject to forces that take them from you. Much of the wealth of that day was in fine clothes, and those were attacked by moths. Some possessions lost value because of **rust.** The word refers to corrosion and also anything that destroys. Everything was subject to **thieves** who sought to take other persons' treasures for themselves. The words **break through** refer to someone digging a hole through the mud dwellings of the poor. Our expression for this would be "break in." Other threats to earthly treasures include recession, unemployment, breakdown of health, accidents, natural disasters, and so forth. In other words, there is no such thing as financial security. This is as true today as it was then. And even when we accumulate possessions on earth, we go with empty hands into eternity (Luke 12:13-21; 16:19-31).

Jesus called His followers to invest earthly resources in the only sure investment—**treasures in heaven.** Money has value in this life. It won't buy everything, but some things can be bought only with money. Yet when we die, we leave it all behind. Although money is a temporal thing, it can be used in such a way as to create eternal things. Money invested in the Lord's work results in saved lives and people's characters changed for eternity.

In verse 21 Jesus linked **treasure** and **heart.** Jesus could have stated this the other way around: "Wherever your heart is, there your treasure will be also." Writers of biographies try to find every possible source that sheds light on a person's life. Cancelled checks and credit card receipts are valuable research sources. These sources show a person's values and priorities. They reveal both heart and treasure.

Verses 22-24: **The light of the body is the eye: if therefore thine eye be single, thy whole body shall be full of light. 23But if thine eye be evil, thy whole body shall be full of darkness. If therefore the light that is in thee be darkness, how great is that darkness! 24No man can serve two masters: for either he will hate the one, and love the other; or else he will hold to the one, and despise the other. Ye cannot serve God and mammon.**

The word **single** translates the Greek word *haplous,* which has several possible meanings—"simple," "single," "whole," "sound" and "good." These different meanings have led to several interpretations. One of these assumes Jesus was speaking of actual eyesight. If your eyesight is good, your **whole body shall be full of light**; if your eyesight is bad, your **whole body shall be full of darkness.** In other words, good eyesight enables a person to see clearly and go about safely. A second interpretation suggests Jesus was contrasting "generous" people with "stingy" people. The generous person sees and acts according to the light. A primary way of laying up treasures in heaven is giving generously to help others. A third interpretation is that Jesus was talking about spiritual vision that leads to single-hearted devotion to God. This person sees life as God sees it.

When I was in the seventh grade, I discovered that I needed glasses. I couldn't read the chalkboard even from the front row. I never will forget the feeling I had when I emerged from the doctor's building wearing my new glasses. The glasses were made to correct my nearsightedness by focusing my vision as it should be. When I looked across the street, I could see the faces of people. I even could see the expressions on their faces, and I could read signs. In that moment, a new world opened up to me. The Lord does the same thing for our spiritual sight. He corrects our blurred vision so we can see physical and spiritual things as they are. He enables us to focus on Him and on the people we are to help.

Verse 24 can stand alone, but its meaning is clearer when studied in context. It is related to the theme of verses 19-34. **Mammon** can be translated "money" (NIV, HCSB). **Mammon** represents preoccupation with and worship of material possessions, for which money is the medium of exchange. Jesus used the word **masters,** referring not to "employers" but to slave owners. The word **serve** occurs twice in the verse, but a more literal translation would be "to serve as a slave." Jesus was talking about a slave who owed total allegiance and total obedience to his master. Jesus' words do not fit our current economic system in which some people work at two jobs with two bosses. Doing two jobs with separate bosses isn't easy, but it is not impossible. Jesus was talking about what is impossible—serving two gods.

Many people then and now make money into a god. Often such people claim to see no contradiction between faith in God and what amounts to worship of material possessions. Those who are preoccupied with money and place their trust in it fail to see that this is a rival religion to the worship of God. People who worship money fail to see that their god is a hard master who exacts a fearful cost. They often discover it too late. The opposite of this is to serve God by laying up treasures in heaven, seeing reality with single-hearted commitment, and worshiping God rather than possessions.

What are some lasting truths in Matthew 6:19-24?

1. Absolute financial security is an illusion.
2. We lay up heavenly treasures when we live by heaven's standards on earth.
3. People who are totally committed to God reveal this by investing their treasures in His kingdom.
4. Single-hearted devotion to God provides a clear vision of reality as God sees it.
5. Total commitment to God is incompatible with selfish, materialistic living.

Trust God for All (Matt. 6:25-32)

*What is meant by **take no thought**? What things do people worry about? What points did Jesus make by mentioning birds and flowers?*

Why is anxiety useless and wrong? How did the teaching of Jesus differ from the practice of the Gentiles?

***Verse 25:* Therefore I say unto you, Take no thought for your life, what ye shall eat, or what ye shall drink; nor yet for your body, what ye shall put on. Is not the life more than meat, and the body than raiment?**

Take no thought is found in some form or other in verses 25,27,28,31, and twice in 34. When the *King James Version* was translated in 1611, the expression "take no thought" carried the idea of anxious thought. But today those words carry a more neutral meaning. Jesus was not forbidding thinking about life or even about planning for the future. The Greek word means "to be anxious" or "to be worried." Thus Jesus condemned anxiety that distracts and paralyzes a person with fear about the unknown future. Jesus used this same word when He told Martha, "You are worried and upset about many things" (Luke 10:41, NIV, HCSB).

In the last part of verse 25, Jesus posed a double question for those who were anxious about life's necessities: **Is not the life more than meat, and the body than raiment?** ("Is not life more important than food, and the body more important than clothes?" NIV). Frederick Dale Bruner well applied Jesus' words to our culture: "The Christian world in the West is on the whole a fat world, too concerned with food; it is a superficial world, too occupied with clothes. Jesus intends to liberate us from these obsession with inanities and to lift our lives to the nobility of caring about things that matter. Our surfeited world must learn that God's gift of **life** is much more important than eating well, and that the gift of the **body** is much more important than dressing well."[1]

***Verses 26-27:* Behold the fowls of the air: for they sow not, neither do they reap, nor gather into barns; yet your heavenly Father feedeth them. Are ye not much better than they? [27]Which of you by taking thought can add one cubit unto his stature?**

Jesus then told His followers, "Look at the birds of the sky" (HCSB). Birds do not sow, reap, or harvest what they plant, yet the Heavenly Father feeds them. Jesus reasoned from the lesser to the greater. If your Heavenly Father feeds the birds of the air (the lesser), surely He will see that you have food (the greater).

Birds are not examples of creatures that simply wait for God to put food in their mouths. They constantly forage for food. God feeds the birds, but He does it by providing a world of food and the means of gathering it and feeding themselves. Thus Jesus was not saying that people should fold their hands and expect God to feed them. The Bible teaches diligence in working to meet our needs and the needs of our families. Idleness is soundly condemned (Prov. 19:15; 2 Thess. 3:11-12). Birds are examples not of idleness but of the absence of anxiety. People of faith still must sow, reap, and store away in barns. They see no contradiction between working and praying, "Give us this day our daily bread."

The word **stature** translates a Greek word that can refer either to height or age. Thus some translations assume that the issue was on of adding height ("Can any of you add a single cubit to his height by worrying?" HCSB); others think that Jesus had in mind adding to the length of life ("Who of you by worrying can add a single hour to his life?" NIV). Most people are more concerned about living longer than getting taller. Either way, no one can get taller or live longer by worrying. In fact, worrying can shorten life by contributing to many health problems.

Verses 28-32: **And why take ye thought for raiment? Consider the lilies of the field, how they grow; they toil not, neither do they spin: [29]And yet I say unto you, That even Solomon in all his glory was not arrayed like one of these. [30]Wherefore, if God so clothe the grass of the field, which today is, and tomorrow is cast into the oven, shall he not much more clothe you, O ye of little faith? [31]Therefore take no thought, saying, What shall we eat? or, What shall we drink? or, Wherewithal shall we be clothed? [32](For after all these things do the Gentiles seek:) for your heavenly Father knoweth that ye have need of all these things.**

With the example of the birds, Jesus dealt with anxiety about food. With the example from **the lilies of the field,** He dealt with anxiety about clothes. The word **lilies** probably referred in a general way to the wild flowers in the land, not to any one species. As the birds did not sow, reap, or gather into barns, the flowers **toil not, neither do they spin.** The word **toil** refers to work in the fields; the word **spin** refers to work done at home to make clothes. Jesus compared the splendor of the flowers to the robes of **Solomon in all his glory.** Solomon in his finest clothes did not have the richness and color of a field of wild flowers.

Verse 30 is another example of arguing from the lesser to the greater: **Wherefore, if God so clothe the grass of the field, which today is, and tomorrow is cast into the oven, shall he not much more clothe you?** The beauty of the wild flowers fades under the withering rays of the sun. The dried flowers and grass are fit only to be burned as fuel. If God gives such beauty to wild flowers (the lesser), surely He can be trusted to provide clothes for His people (the greater)?

Jesus spoke of those who have **little faith.** He did not say they had no faith, only little faith. They believed in Him, but their faith needed to grow and become more mature. Jesus knew that His disciples were pilgrims of faith. They were on their way but not yet there. He knew that the world often tempted even the strongest of them to fall into the subtle snare of anxiety. They required constant reminding that they needed divine guidance and strength to avoid this sin.

Jesus' Sermon on the Mount is a call to live by the standards of God's eternal kingdom. Therefore, He warned His hearers against becoming like the secular world and the hypocritical religious leaders. Jesus challenged the ways of the world and the practices of the religious world. One of Jesus' arguments against anxiety was that it was the way of **the Gentiles.** They were tempted to forsake the way of faith for **all these things** that **the Gentiles seek.** Pagan unbelievers worry about what they will eat or drink and what they will wear. Thus anxiety is wrong not only because it is useless but because it is dangerous and pagan.

Christians need not seek these things the way pagans do, because they know their **heavenly Father** knows they **have need of all these things.**

What are some lasting truths in Matthew 6:25-32?

1. Jesus' followers should not be anxious about food or clothing.
2. Life is more than possessions.
3. Anxiety is useless, dangerous, and pagan.
4. Since God provides food for birds and clothes the flowers with beauty, surely He will feed and clothe His people.
5. Anxiety about material things reveals how little faith and trust in God we have.

Seek God Before All (Matt. 6:33-34)

Why is verse 33 a key verse? Why would followers of Jesus need to be told this? What is the significance of key words in verse 33? What contribution does verse 34 make?

Verses 33-34: **But seek ye first the kingdom of God, and his righteousness; and all these things shall be added unto you. [34]Take therefore no thought for the morrow: for the morrow shall take thought for the things of itself. Sufficient unto the day is the evil thereof.**

Verse 33 is the key verse in the Sermon on the Mount, and perhaps in the Gospel of Matthew. Some people use this verse as an invitation to enter the kingdom, but more likely it was addressed to those committed to Him but needing to grow morally and spiritually. Why would committed disciples need to be told this? In spite of our commitment to Christ, we are tempted to live by the world's standards. And nothing is more worldly than preoccupation with selfish acquisition of things.

Nearly every word in the verse is important. **Seek** contrasts this verse to verse 32, which mentions the things the Gentiles seek. The Gentiles seek treasures on earth and are anxious to get them and hold on to them. Their goals in life are focused on material things for themselves.

To the contrary, the goal and driving force for believers should be **the kingdom of God, and his righteousness. The kingdom of God** refers to the present and future reign of God. He already has revealed His sovereignty through Christ. He has promised that one day every knee will bow and every tongue confess that Jesus is Lord to the glory of God (Phil. 2:10-11). Meanwhile we live in a world that has different standards than God's kingdom. Believers pray that God will bring in His kingdom, and they seek to live by the high standards of His eternal kingdom.

Righteousness also refers to the present and the future. God's righteousness is first of all the right standing He gives us through faith in Christ; it also is the righteousness He creates in believers through His Spirit. Believers **seek . . . his righteousness** in the sense of hungering for it.

Notice that it is His **kingdom** and **righteousness,** not ours. They become ours only as we honor Him. This is where the word **first** applies. **First** can refer to first in a sequence of time or first in the sense of foremost in priority. Both fit the context and are consistent with Jesus' teachings. Luke 9:57-62 tells of three would-be followers. The first one had not put Jesus first in importance. The other two had something they wanted to do first before following Jesus. Combining both meanings, Jesus called people to follow Him first and to give Him first place in their lives.

All these things shall be added unto you provides another link with verse 32. Jesus' promise is to all whose consuming ambition is God's kingdom and righteousness. **All these things** refer to all the things mentioned in verse 31, which include food and clothing. These are things God's people need to do His will. God promises to provide all we **need** to do His will, not all the things we may want. Our society has taken the list of real needs and gradually convinced many people that the things we *want* are things we *need.*

Some corollary truths come to mind. One is that God expects us to do our part. Another is that God often meets human needs through the efforts of others. We cannot be content with having our personal needs met. God expects us to be generous in sharing with those who lack basic necessities (Matt. 25:35-36).

Verse 34 is a summary verse on the anxiety theme in this passage. Worries are basically fears of what may happen in an unknown future. Thus anxiety is nearly always about **the morrow.** Many fears are about tomorrow, but today is the only day in which we live. When concerns about tomorrow drain our energies, we are not able to focus on the only time we have—today. The fact is, **Sufficient unto the day is the evil thereof,** or in more modern language, "Each day has enough trouble of its own" (NIV, HCSB). If we spend our time worrying about what may happen tomorrow, we will worry about many things that never happen and we will weaken our ability to deal with tomorrow's problems if and when they do happen.

What are some lasting truths in Matthew 6:33-34?

1. God will supply the needs of those who first seek God and His ways.
2. Worry prevents Jesus' followers from devoting themselves to God and His concerns.
3. We are to meet each day's troubles as they come and not be distracted by tomorrow's possible troubles that may never come.

❖ *Spiritual Transformations*

In His sermon Jesus told His followers to lay up treasures in heaven, not on earth; to have single-hearted devotion to God; that they cannot worship God and money at the same time; that they should not be anxious about having the necessities of life; and that those who trust God and put Him first will receive what they need to do His will.

Why do many people worry so much? ______________________

____

Why do you *worry so much?* ______________________

____

What are some cures for worry? ______________________

Prayer of Commitment: Lord, forgive my worrying and help me put first things first for You and Your kingdom. Amen.

[1]Frederick Dale Bruner, *The Christbook: Matthew 1–12* [Waco: Word Books, 1987], 266.

Week of November 18

20/20 VISION

Bible Passage: Matthew 7:1-12

❖ *Significance of the Lesson*

• The *Life Question* is, As a follower of Jesus, how should I relate to others?

• The *Biblical Truth* is that for followers of Jesus, knowing God as Father helps them develop properly focused attitudes toward themselves, God, and others.

• The *Life Impact* is designed to help you live as a follower of Jesus by realizing that life with God is relational and then committing to show God's love in your dealings with others.

Relationship Problems

Humanity has made tremendous strides forward in science and technology. The most striking of these have been made during the lifetimes of adults who are living today. Yet during this same time we have made little progress in being able to relate to fellow human beings. Modern times have experienced wars that killed and maimed millions. Terrorism and crime seem to grow stronger and more brazen. Some relationship problems are closer to home. Sometimes adults may feel that broken and strained relationships are normal. Their marriage relationship is on the rocks. Their teens live in their own faraway world. Neighbors next door don't speak with them anymore. And even their relationship with God has soured. How can we move from these bad relations to good relations with God and others? This lesson focuses on the answer to this question.

Word Study: *Judge*

The Greek word *krino* in Matthew 7:1 has a number of possible meanings. It can refer to a legal action in a judicial setting or to the judgment of God, the ultimate Judge. On a personal level it can refer to finding fault with another person and even condemning the person.

In the more neutral sense the word can refer to carefully considering or even expressing a preference.

❖ *Search the Scriptures*

Jesus warned His disciples against judging others. He said they would be judged for judging. He showed how ridiculous and inconsistent it is to see the faults of others while remaining blind to one's own sins. Judging is wrong, but judgments made based on evaluation of others are necessary. Jesus encouraged persistent praying to the Father, who will answer prayer. Jesus gave the Golden Rule to guide His followers in how they should act toward others.

See Yourself More Clearly (Matt. 7:1-6)

What kinds of judging are not covered in verse 1 and what kinds are covered? With what ***measure*** *shall we* ***be judged****? How do verses 3-4 show the folly of one sinner judging another? What kind of people did Jesus call* ***hypocrite****? How does verse 6 qualify verses 1-5?*

Verses 1-2: **Judge not, that ye be not judged. [2]For with what judgment ye judge, ye shall be judged: and with what measure ye mete, it shall be measured to you again.**

Frederick Dale Bruner wrote of these verses: "This is simply the fifth Blessing in summary and in reverse, 'Blessed are the merciful, for they will receive mercy.' 'Don't judge' also summarizes the content of the . . . commands in the heart of chapter 5 concerning anger, revenge, and hate. 'Don't judge' recapitulates in fresh language the fifth petition of the Lord's Prayer in the middle of chapter 6: 'forgive us our debts, as we have forgiven our debtors.' In a way, then, the command not to judge summarizes the heart of both the preceding chapters."[1]

When He talked about judging others, Jesus dealt with a sin to which many religious people are tempted. We need to understand what Jesus did not mean in order to clarify what He did mean. Three misunderstandings confuse the issue. First, Jesus was not forbidding legal processes that involve judges and courts. This was a misunderstanding championed by Leo Tolstoy, the Russian novelist who wrote *War and Peace.* He saw the Sermon on the Mount as a blueprint for society and thus verse 1 literally applying to all human judging. Yet the Old Testament commanded that judges settle disputes and render judgments against crimes (Ex. 18:17-23). The judges were warned to be impartial but to serve the community and God by fulfilling their role as judges (2 Chron. 19:5-7). The New Testament recognizes that those who enforce the law for the community are ordained by God to protect people and punish criminals (Rom. 13:1-7).

A second misunderstanding is that Jesus was forbidding any moral evaluations. God's people at times must make value judgments by discerning between truth and error, good and evil. The Sermon on the Mount assumes that Christ's followers can distinguish God's righteousness from the righteousness of the Pharisees and the practices of pagan people. In 7:6 Jesus commanded the disciples to distinguish people of faith from people whom He compared to dogs and pigs. Later in chapter 7 Jesus warned against false teachers, who could be recognized by their fruit (7:15-20).

Third, Jesus was not telling His disciples never to identify and condemn evil. Later in Matthew Jesus set up a process for church discipline (18:15-17). Paul instructed the Corinthian church to deal with a case of notorious immorality among their members (1 Cor. 5:1-5).

A thin line exists between obeying biblical teachings about condemning evil and biblical warnings against judging others. What determines the difference? Basically, Jesus was condemning people who forget that they too are sinners accountable to God and act as if they are God the Judge. We commit the sin of judging when we act as if we were God and pass final judgment on others.

In verse 2 Jesus warned people who judge others that they will be judged: **For with what judgment ye judge, ye shall be judged.** Only God is qualified to be Judge in the ultimate sense. There are two major reasons for this. For one thing, only God has all the facts needed to render judgment on a person. He knows all our actions—public and private. He knows our thoughts and the intents of our hearts. None of us has such knowledge of another person—however well we think we know the person. The only exercise some people get is jumping to conclusions. They see or hear about certain actions, and they make certain assumptions about their meaning. This is why gossip is so deadly. It is based on these assumptions. Gossip is among the most common sins of church people.

The other reason why only God is qualified to be Judge is that only He has the character needed by the Judge of all humanity: **Ye shall be judged: and with what measure ye mete, it shall be measured to you again** ("You will be judged, and with the measure you use, it will be measured to you," NIV, HCSB). Only God has the justice and mercy needed by the Judge. Human judgments are often unjust and unmerciful. Jesus' disciples James and John provide a good example. They asked Jesus to call down fire on a Samaritan village. Instead, Jesus rebuked them for their harsh spirit (Luke 9:52-56). When others judge us, we can take comfort that our ultimate judgment is in the hands of God, not in their hands (1 Cor. 4:3-5).

The kind of judgment Jesus condemned can be described as judgmentalism or censoriousness. "Censoriousness is a compound sin consisting of several unpleasant ingredients. It does not mean to assess people critically, but to judge them harshly. The censorious critic is a fault-finder who is negative and destructive towards other people and enjoys actively seeking out their failings. He puts the worst possible construction on their motives, pours cold water on their schemes and is ungenerous towards their mistakes."[2]

The judgment Jesus condemned is harsh, unsympathetic, and unmerciful. People who show mercy and forgiveness toward others have experienced God's mercy and forgiveness in their own lives. If we rely on God's mercy, then we must share it as well as receive it. If a person has a harsh judgmental spirit, such a person shall be judged by the same harsh and judgmental standards by which he has judged others.

Verses 3-5: **And why beholdest thou the mote that is in thy brother's eye, but considerest not the beam that is in thine own eye? 4Or how wilt thou say to thy brother, Let me pull out the mote out of thine eye; and, behold, a beam is in thine own eye? 5Thou hypocrite, first cast out the beam out of thine own eye; and then shalt thou see clearly to cast out the mote out of thy brother's eye.**

The word picture of these verses is ridiculous in its exaggeration, but Jesus' point is memorable and clear. In verse 3 Jesus asked why a person with a **beam** ("plank," NIV; "log," HCSB) in his **eye** would point to a **mote** ("speck," NIV, HCSB) in his brother's eye. The person sees the speck in his brother's eye but is unable to see the large log in his own eye. The obvious point is that we are more sensitive to the sins of others than we are to our own sins. Our sins may be far worse than theirs, but we see their sins while remaining blind to our own enormous evils.

Jesus condemned such a judgmental person as a **hypocrite,** a play actor hiding behind a mask. He told the disciples, **First cast out the beam out of thine own eye; and then shalt thou see clearly to cast out the mote out of thy brother's eye.** This sentence has two parts.

First, we are to deal with our own sins. Then we are to help others with their sins. This involves redemptive discipline. Paul wrote, "Brothers, if someone is caught in any wrongdoing, you who are spiritual should restore such a person with a gentle spirit, watching out for yourselves so you won't be tempted also" (Gal. 6:1, HCSB; see also Matt. 18:15-17; 2 Cor. 2:5-11). The goal of such discipline is forgiveness and reconciliation. But the person who takes the initiative should always remember that he too is a sinner.

Verse 6: **Give not that which is holy unto the dogs, neither cast ye your pearls before swine, lest they trample them under their feet, and turn again and rend you.**

The dogs of that time were not domesticated pets who were man's best friend. They were wild dogs that ran in packs of scavengers. **Swine** ("pigs," NIV, HCSB) were considered by the Jews to be the epitome of unclean things. No one gave **holy** things to wild dogs. The dogs, after tearing up the holy things, would turn on the person and tear him apart. Similarly, no one **cast . . . pearls before swine** as they would **trample them under their feet, and turn again and rend you.**

What kinds of people are represented by **the dogs** and the **swine**? What kinds of things are represented as **that which is holy** and as **pearls**? Most Bible students think the holy things and pearls represent the gospel message and the dogs and pigs represent people who are hostile to Christ and would trash the gospel message.

If discernment in sharing the gospel is what Jesus meant, we must be careful about how we apply this principle. The basic thrust of the New Testament is for us to share the good news with all people. Add to this the fact that none of us knows who is so lost that he or she is irreparably lost. Think of all the missionaries and persecuted believers who have labored for years in the face of continual rejection and hostility. After years of continual hostility, some people are converted. John Stott reminded us that choosing to not tell the good news to anyone should be a rare occurrence. "I can think of only one or two occasions in my experience when I felt it was right. This teaching of Jesus is for exceptional situations only; our normal Christian duty is to be patient and persevere with others, as God has patiently persevered with us."[3]

What are some lasting truths in Matthew 7:1-6?

1. People who judge others will themselves be judged—and according to the same standard with which they have judged others.
2. Only God has the knowledge and character to be Judge.

3. People often see the sins of others but are blind to their own sins.
4. Don't be judgmental, but also don't fail to discern evil.

See God More Clearly (Matt. 7:7-11)

Why is 7:7-8 one of the best prayer promises in the Bible? Why is persistent praying important? Why is trust in God as Father crucial for praying?

Verses 7-8: **Ask, and it shall be given you; seek, and ye shall find; knock, and it shall be opened unto you: [8]For everyone that asketh receiveth; and he that seeketh findeth; and to him that knocketh it shall be opened.**

The Sermon on the Mount is filled with challenges to genuine Christian living. The high demands of chapters 5–6 are matched by the words of 7:1-6. How can we live up to such high demands? The answer is in 7:7-11, through a life of prayer. Earlier, in the Model Prayer (6:9-13), Jesus taught His disciples how to pray; in 7:7-11 He encouraged them to have a life of prayer.

The Bible is filled with promises that God hears and answers real prayers. This is one of the greatest of these promises. Our prayers are described by three words—**ask . . . seek . . . knock.** These words are not an unconditional promise that God will give us everything we want. The promise is contingent on a right relationship with God, and the goal is the coming of God's kingdom and glory. God has the riches of His power and love ready to pour out on those who **ask** for them—**ask, and it shall be given you.** We ask, believing God will give us what we need, not everything we want. **Seek** is the same word that was used in 6:32 for what worldly people seek and in 6:33 of seeking first God's kingdom of righteousness. The word **knock** is used to climax the threefold promise. It is the image of a door being opened to allow one to enter.

Actually each of the three key words is in a Greek tense that refers to ongoing actions: "Keep asking, and it will be given to you. Keep seeking, and you will find. Keep knocking, and the door will be opened to you" (HCSB). Jesus warned against using many words in prayers as pagans do (6:6). The pagan prayers repeat set phrases over and over, thinking this will get the attention of their gods and show how pious they are. But Jesus taught persistent praying, as is shown in two of His parables (Luke 11:8-11; 18:1-8).

Verses 9-11: **Or what man is there of you, whom if his son ask bread, will he give him a stone? [10]Or if he ask a fish, will he give him a serpent? [11]If ye then, being evil, know how to give good gifts unto your children, how much more shall your Father which is in heaven give good things to them that ask him?**

Earlier Jesus stressed that God knows our needs before we ask (6:8,32). In 7:11 Jesus told believers to continue to pray and ask God to meet those needs. God is our Father. He will not give us anything bad, only what is good. If a child asked his father for **bread,** would **he give him a stone?** If the child asked for **a fish,** would his father **give him a serpent?** If imperfect earthly fathers seek **to give good gifts unto** their **children,** then **how much more shall** the **Father which is in heaven give good things to them that ask him?** As noted earlier, the most important fact about prayer is the God to whom we pray. And our prayers are lifted up to our Heavenly Father, who loves us and wants to answer our prayers.

Real prayer is persistent because: (1) We have real needs that only God can meet. We live in a world of needs that only He can meet. (2) Prayer is essentially fellowship with God. A personal relationship calls for spending time together. (3) Persistent prayer changes those who pray. (4) God uses our prayers to work out His will in us and in the lives of others.

What are some lasting truths in Matthew 7:7-11?

1. God promises to respond to our prayers when we keep on asking, seeking, and knocking, that is, when we are persistent in our prayers.
2. If imperfect earthly fathers give good things to their children, how much more will the Heavenly Father give good things to His children?

See Others More Clearly (Matt. 7:12)

How is the Golden Rule sometimes stated negatively? Why did Jesus use the positive statement? Why is it risky to practice the Golden Rule?

Verse 12: **Therefore all things whatsoever ye would that men should do to you, do ye even so to them: for this is the law and the prophets.**

Life's relationships include God and others. The world focuses on selfish personal needs and wants. The Bible reminds us that we must love others. The Golden Rule is another way of stating what Jesus said was the basic Old Testament way of relating to other people: "Love thy neighbor as thyself" (Lev. 19:18; Matt. 22:39). How can we achieve this kind of love? The Golden Rule tells how: "Whatever you want others to do for you, do also the same for them" (HCSB).

People sometimes claim that Jesus was only one of many teachers and philosophers to state the Golden Rule. There were in fact a host of others who set forth a negative form of the Golden Rule—this is sometimes called the Silver Rule. It goes something like this: "Don't do to others what you don't want them to do to you." Among those who stated such a rule were Confucius, Rabbi Hillel, and the Stoic philosophers. Archibald Hunter pointed out the contrast between these statements and Jesus' statement: "All these are negative, and in the negative form the conduct called for need not rise much above a calculating prudence anxious to avoid trouble. Christ's Rule is positive. He insists not merely that we do not do evil to another but that we do him active good. . . . We are to treat others with the same considerateness we would like them to show to us."[4]

Hans Dieter Betz further pointed out: "The Golden Rule demands a willingness to take considerable risks. One has no guarantee that people will respond in kind when approached with generosity and goodwill. While it is considered realistic and prudent to act in this way, because human beings behave accordingly most of the time and because it is the right way of acting, one has no assurance that they will do so all of the time. Indeed, there is plenty of evidence that humans can be unfair, ungrateful, exploitative, cynical, and brutal, no matter how kindly one may treat them."[5]

When the good Samaritan stopped to help the injured man, he was risking his own life. The thieves might still have been lurking nearby. But the Samaritan knew that if he were the injured man, he would want someone to stop and help him. The priest and Levite played it safe. They passed by on the other side (Luke 10:30-37). They did not practice the Golden Rule; the Samaritan did.

What are some lasting truths in Matthew 7:12?

1. The negative form of the Golden Rule could lead a person to do nothing in a time of need.

2. The positive form of the Golden Rule that Jesus taught calls for action to meet the needs of others.

❖ *Spiritual Transformations*

In this portion of the Sermon on the Mount, Jesus focused on human relations. He began by warning against the sin of passing judgment on other people. Only God is qualified to be Judge because only He knows all the facts and only He has the character to judge with justice and mercy. Although judging is wrong when done the wrong way, judgments based on evaluation are necessary to avoid giving holy things to people who act like wild dogs and pigs. Meanwhile, we must maintain a right relation with God through prayer. If earthly fathers give good things to their children, how much more will our Heavenly Father do for those who ask, seek, and knock? The Golden Rule is the Christian way of acting for the good of others.

To a great extent life is about relationships. We relate to many people and in a variety of ways—parents, siblings, playmates, teachers, school mates, church leaders, spouses, children, in-laws, employers, fellow workers, neighbors, and friends. We relate well or poorly. We build solid foundations, and we suffer strained or broken relationships. A top priority for Christians should be to relate well to God, to other believers, and to all people. To do this takes concentrated effort, but wholesome relationships are worth the expenditure of time and energy.

*How do you show your commitment to love others?*____________

____

Prayer of Commitment: Lord, help me relate to others as Jesus did and taught. Amen.

[1]Bruner, *The Christbook: Matthew 1–12*, 272.

[2]Stott, *The Message of the Sermon on the Mount*, 176.

[3]Stott, *The Message of the Sermon on the Mount*, 183.

[4]Archibald M. Hunter, *A Pattern for Life*, revised edition [Philadelphia: Westminster Press, 1965], 90-91.

[5]Hans Dieter Betz, *The Sermon on the Mount*, in Hermeneia—A Critical and Historical Commentary on the Bible [Minneapolis: Fortress Press, 1995], 519.

Week of November 25

MAKE UP YOUR MINDS

Bible Passage: Matthew 7:13-29

❖ *Significance of the Lesson*

- The *Life Question* is, Have I decided to follow Jesus Christ?
- The *Biblical Truth* is that those who choose to believe in Jesus and follow His teachings experience new life now and forever.
- The *Life Impact* is designed to help you live as a follower of Jesus by affirming that believing in Jesus and following His teachings are choices and then helping you to make those choices.
- This is the **Evangelism Lesson** for this quarter.

Crucial Decisions

As a rule, adults are more reluctant than children and youth to make public professions of faith. They are often too concerned about what people will think of someone who is so late in coming to Christ. But examples of adults following Jesus are found throughout the Bible and human history. This is the most crucial decision anyone, whatever his or her age, can make. At the end of the Sermon on the Mount, Jesus invited His hearers to commit to Him and to walk in His way.

Evangelistic Invitations

When I was a child, my family attended a church of a different denomination than Baptists. Whenever I attended church with a Baptist friend or relative, I was impressed by the fact that after every sermon there was an evangelistic invitation. No service closed without a call to receive Jesus Christ as Savior. Baptists and other evangelical churches are surely being true to the Bible by having a time of decision in the service. Billy Graham has used an evangelistic invitation in his crusades. Multitudes have made life-changing commitments during these invitation times. We have a strong biblical support for doing this. At the end of the Sermon on the Mount, Jesus extended an evangelistic invitation. He included not only a call to choose the door of salvation but also a challenge to walk the Christian walk.

Word Study: *Authority*

The word *exousia* in Matthew 7:28 has the idea of power as well as authority. This probably means that Jesus did not quote previous teachers for authority as the scribes did. He spoke with the power and authority of the Son of God.

❖ *Search the Scriptures*

In the final part of the Sermon on the Mount Jesus challenged people to decision and action. He invited His hearers to enter the narrow gate of salvation and walk the difficult way of discipleship. He warned of false prophets who could be recognized by their fruits and of professing believers who lack a personal knowledge of Him. He challenged all who heard the Word to obey it, lest the storms of life overwhelm them.

The three outline points indicate three areas about you need to, as the lesson title states, *Make Up Your Minds.*

About Life's Directions (Matt. 7:13-14)

What four pairs of things did Jesus contrast? What words describe each of these? How do these verses constitute an invitation? How do they challenge disciples?

Verses 13-14: **Enter ye in at the strait gate: for wide is the gate, and broad is the way, that leadeth to destruction, and many there be which go in thereat: [14]Because strait is the gate, and narrow is the way, which leadeth unto life, and few there be that find it.**

In these verses Jesus contrasted two gates, two roads, two crowds, and two destinations. A **gate** is a door or entryway into something. One gate Jesus called **strait** (notice the spelling of the word). Some people assume Jesus said "straight," but the old *King James Version* word **strait** means "narrow" (NIV, HCSB). The narrow gate signifies entrance into salvation. If salvation is free, why did Jesus refer to the entrance as narrow? Although salvation is the gift of God's grace to believers, receiving it demands repentance and commitment. The gate is narrow because many people shrink from repentance and commitment.

By contrast the other gate is **wide** because it represents the easy way of drifting through life and failing to enter the narrow gate.

The narrow gate leads to the **narrow . . . way.** The word translated **narrow** in verse 14b is different from the word rendered "narrow" by the newer translations in verse 13. This word can be translated "difficult" (HCSB). The word **way** refers figuratively to a "road" (NIV, HCSB). The contrasting pictures are of a narrow gate that leads to a difficult road and a wide gate that leads to a **broad** road.

Frederick Dale Bruner correctly pointed out the significance of Jesus' exhortation: "Jesus is appealing *both* for an evangelical decision (the gate) *and* for an ethical endurance (the way). Taken together, then, the narrow gate and the tough way are simply the difficult choice for Jesus *and* the constantly challenging decisions for discipleship to him."[1] Combining the calls to salvation and discipleship shows the close connection between salvation and discipleship.

The two crowds are the kinds of people on each of the two roads. Christians have entered the narrow gate and are living the way of the cross, which is difficult in a world where so many are walking on the broad, easy road of worldly living. Jesus said that only a **few** find the way of Christ, but **many** are traveling the broad way of the world. We probably should not use this passage to speculate about how many or how few will be saved but to be sure we have entered the narrow door.

Each of these roads leads to a different destination. The narrow gate and the hard road lead to **life.** The wide gate and broad way lead to **destruction.** People need not wait to discover their destination. Heaven is at the end of the difficult road, and hell is at the end of an uncommitted life. As you make up your mind about directions, be sure you are on the road that leads to life.

In his classic allegory of salvation and the Christian life, John Bunyan wrote of a man under conviction of sin who wanted to leave the city of destruction and journey to the celestial city. He met a man called Evangelist, who pointed him to a wicket gate. Entering it did not mean the end but the beginning of a life of joys and troubles. Nevertheless, he followed that road to heaven.

What are some lasting truths in Matthew 7:13-14?

1. The door to salvation is narrow because it demands repentance and commitment.

2. The way of Jesus is hard because it runs counter to the way of the world.

3. Those who fail to enter the narrow door drift through the wide door.
4. Many drift along the broad road, but few walk the hard road.
5. One's ultimate destiny depends on which door one entered and which road one follows.

About Life's Influences (Matt. 7:15-23)

*Why are **false prophets** deceptive and dangerous? How can Christians identify false prophets? How can we reconcile verses 15-20 with verses 1-5? Are the people of verses 21-23 the same as those in verses 15-20? How did the Lord deny their claim? How can we reconcile verses 21-23 with Romans 10:13?*

Verses 15-20: **Beware of false prophets, which come to you in
sheep's clothing, but inwardly they are ravening wolves. 16Ye shall
know them by their fruits. Do men gather grapes of thorns, or figs
of thistles? 17Even so every good tree bringeth forth good fruit; but
a corrupt tree bringeth forth evil fruit. 18A good tree cannot bring
forth evil fruit, neither can a corrupt tree bring forth good fruit.
19Every tree that bringeth not forth good fruit is hewn down, and
cast into the fire. 20Wherefore by their fruits ye shall know them.**

Some Bible students believe that verses 15-20 and 21-23 refer to the same group, but many think they are two different groups. Verses 15-20 refer to false prophets who are wolves disguised as sheep. Verses 21-23 refer to professing believers who claim to have worked miracles in God's name. Verses 15-20 focus on people who try to disguise themselves as sheep; verses 21-23 focus on those who think they are true followers but are not.

Jesus warned against **false prophets.** Jeremiah condemned false prophets for leading people astray, for raising false hopes, and for speaking their own words while claiming to speak for God (Jer. 23:9-23). The New Testament warns against false prophets (Matt. 7:15-20), false teachers (2 Pet. 2:1), false apostles (2 Cor. 11:13), and even of false Christs (Matt. 24:24). All of these posed a threat to believers, and their claims were lies.

These false prophets would appear **in sheep's clothing.** They would not appear to be outsiders who pose a threat to the church. On the surface they would appear to be among the true sheep of God's flock. This deception would make them dangerous. All their claims would be lies because they would not actually be sheep but **ravening** ("ravaging," HCSB; "ferocious," NIV) **wolves.** Paul too warned the leaders of the church at Ephesus that after his departure "savage wolves will come in among you, not sparing the flock" (Acts 20:29, HCSB).

How can believers distinguish true and false prophets? Jesus answered this question: **Ye shall know them by their fruits.** A wolf may disguise itself as a sheep, but eventually its wolf nature will be evident. Jesus used the analogy of fruit bearing. **Thorns** do not produce **grapes,** but more thorns. The same applies to **figs** and **thistles.** Jesus moved from kinds of trees in verse 16 to qualities of trees and their fruit in verses 17-18. Jesus was using fruit in a figurative way. He contrasted **good fruit** with **evil** ("bad," NIV, HCSB) **fruit.**

What are examples of the evil fruit of false prophets? One obvious fruit is the quality of their lives. Paul contrasted the works of the flesh with the fruit of the Spirit (Gal. 5:19-23). This test is not just for false prophets but for all believers. Do our lives show the fruit of the Spirit or the works of the flesh? We need to hold ourselves and our fellow believers accountable for this.

Another kind of evil fruit of false teachers is what they teach. Prophets claim to speak the truth of God. False prophets tend to distort the truth of God's Word. John warned against those who denied basic truths of the Christian faith (1 John 4:1-3). Paul had no patience with those who preached a false gospel (Gal. 1:6-9). We have the Bible as our sole rule of faith and practice. We should study it for many reasons, one of which is to recognize false prophets by their teaching.

Another test of a religious leader is the long-range impact of his ministry. Are lost people saved, and do they grow to become mature disciples? A word of caution is in order. *Fruit* is not always the same thing as *results.* Many false leaders know how to get results by using certain methods. Deuteronomy 13:1-5 describes a prophet who performed what appeared to be miracles, but the prophet led people astray. In Matthew 7:22-23 Jesus told of people who worked miracles but who did not know Him. Many people are too easily impressed by what seem to be graphic evidences of God's work. The real test is not the spectacular but the long-range effect of a ministry.

Is Matthew 7:15-20 in conflict with verses 1-5? No, these verses do not address the kind of judging Jesus condemned at the start of the chapter. How then can we be "fruit inspectors" without setting ourselves up as self-righteous judges? In verses 1-5 Jesus warned against harsh, judgmental, and self-righteous people, who are quick to pass judgment on others based on inadequate information. This warning in verses 15-20 does not rule out the necessary exercise of careful discernment when evaluating the claims of someone who claims he speaks for God.

Verses 21-23: **Not everyone that saith unto me, Lord, Lord, shall enter into the kingdom of heaven; but he that doeth the will of my Father which is in heaven. [22]Many will say to me in that day, Lord, Lord, have we not prophesied in thy name? and in thy name have cast out devils? and in thy name done many wonderful works? [23]And then will I profess unto them, I never knew you: depart from me, ye that work iniquity.**

Verses 21-23 seem to refer to people other than the false prophets described in verses 15-20. The false prophets knew they were not members of God's flock but wolves in sheep's clothing. The people in verses 21-23 sincerely thought they were among God's people. They called Jesus **Lord, Lord.** In other words, they had made a public profession of faith. Elsewhere in the Bible is the promise, "Whosoever shall call upon the name of the Lord shall be saved" (Rom. 10:13; see also Joel 2:32; Acts 2:21). Paul said that faith in the heart is expressed by confession with the mouth (Rom. 10:9). Yet in Matthew 7:21 Jesus said, **Not everyone that saith unto me, Lord, Lord, shall enter into the kingdom of heaven; but he that doeth the will of my Father which is in heaven.** Was Jesus saying that people are saved by doing good works? No. The New Testament consistently proclaims salvation by grace through faith; however, it also consistently teaches that real faith shows itself in good works. These are the *fruit,* not the *root* of salvation. When people claim to be saved but their lives are disobedient to God, their confession is called into question.

Nevertheless, these people will ask on the **day** of judgment, **Lord, Lord, have we not prophesied in thy name? and in thy name have cast out devils? and in thy name done many wonderful works?** They had done more than profess faith in Jesus; they also performed **many wonderful works** in Jesus' **name.** Frederick Dale Bruner suggested that these people were too impressed with what they had done. The three things they mentioned were outwardly impressive, but "the fruits Jesus commanded in this sermon are much less sensational and much simpler: revering Scripture's commands, the casting out of one's own anger, the miracles of sexual purity and marital fidelity, the spiritual speech that does not overuse God's name and that does not defame the other person, and most deeply, the heart that extends itself even to persecutors and enemies."[2]

Jesus gave three reasons for excluding these people from heaven. One of these was their failure to do **the will of** the **Father.** Whatever they professed, they did not do the will of the Father. In Luke 6:46 Jesus asked, "Why do you call Me 'Lord, Lord,' and don't do the things I say?" (HCSB). Professing Jesus as Lord means that He is our Master, to whom we owe absolute loyalty and obedience. Continually disobeying what the Lord said is the Father's will calls in question the validity of the profession.

The second reason for their exclusion is that Jesus said, **I never knew you.** He never knew them because they never knew Him. This is a devastating judgment. They had professed Him as Lord, but they never had that personal knowledge of Him that is the heart of genuine faith.

The third reason for their exclusion was that they were doing evil: **Depart from me, ye that work iniquity.** In spite of their professed faith and service for the Lord, Jesus called them evildoers. This shows that assurance of salvation cannot be based solely on one's profession of faith or on what someone thinks he or she does in service for the Lord.

What are some lasting truths in Matthew 7:15-23?

1. False prophets are deceptive and dangerous, and we should beware of them.
2. Evaluate people who claim to speak for God by how they live and by what they say.
3. Be a "fruit inspector" when necessary, but avoid being harsh and judgmental.
4. Assurance of salvation cannot be based merely one's profession of faith or on what one believes he or she does for the Lord.
5. Some self-confident people will be excluded on the day of judgment.
6. Every one of us should be sure we know the Son and obey the Father.

About Life's Foundations (Matt. 7:24-29)

How were the two houses in Jesus' parable alike? How were they different? What point was Jesus making in the parable of verses 24-27? How was Jesus' teaching different from the teachings of the scribes?

Verses 24-27: **Therefore whosoever heareth these sayings of mine, and doeth them, I will liken him unto a wise man, which built**

his house upon a rock: [25]And the rain descended, and the floods came, and the winds blew, and beat upon that house; and it fell not: for it was founded upon a rock. [26]And everyone that heareth these sayings of mine, and doeth them not, shall be likened unto a foolish man, which built his house upon the sand: [27]and the rain descended, and the floods came, and the winds blew, and beat upon that house; and it fell: and great was the fall of it.

Jesus' last challenge in the Sermon on the Mount comes in His parable of the two houses. **Heareth** ("hears," NIV, HCSB) and **doeth** ("acts on them," HCSB, "puts them into practice," NIV) are the key words. "Hear," when used in this way, assumes the hearer will also heed what he hears, hence the close connection between hearing and doing.

Jesus had just spoken the greatest of His teachings. He referred back to them as **these sayings of mine.** Now in His final words of the sermon Jesus called on His hearers to do more than to hear—He called on them to do what He said.

Jesus compared a person who put into practice His teachings to **a wise man, which built his house upon a rock.** The word **wise** refers to a thoughtful, practical person of good judgment and common sense. He was wise because he **built his house upon a rock.** As verses 26-27 show, this was not the only possible building site available. The surface was sandy and rocky, but often down below was a ledge of rock. The wise man was smart enough to dig down to a ledge of rock as the site for his house. Luke 6:48 gives more details about this: "He is like a man which built an house, and digged down deep, and laid the foundation on a rock." After his house was built, it probably looked like the other house in verses 26-27.

What did the rock foundation represent? Jesus said that it was putting into practice the things He had taught them. Of course in back of putting Jesus' teachings into practice lies a commitment to Jesus as Lord that leads a person to practice His teachings. Ultimately then Jesus is the foundation on which the wise man built his house and lived his life.

The first man was wise and foresighted enough to know that storms come and that only a house built on the rock could survive a severe storm. Water was scarce in that land. When the snow melted in the mountains or the fall rains came, flash floods were not uncommon. And so, **the rain descended, and the floods came, and the winds blew, and beat upon that house; and it fell not: for it was founded upon a rock.**

What do the storms represent? Jesus referred to judgment on "that day" in verse 22, so Jesus could have had the judgment in mind; however, He probably was thinking about the storms of life that come to all people. Notice that both houses were battered by the same storm described by the same words.

The other man in the parable **built his house upon the sand.** He did not go to the time and expense of digging down to a rock ledge. As we noted, the two houses probably looked alike from the outside, but the second house had no solid foundation. The man who built the second house Jesus called **foolish** because he did not take into account the effect of a storm on a house built on sand. He had no foresight. As the parable unfolded, Jesus used the same words to describe the storm that hammered the house built on the sand. The effect of the storm on the second house was total destruction: **It fell: and great was the fall of it** ("it fell with a great crash," NIV).

There was only one difference between the two houses—the foundation. There was one main difference between the two men. The wise man heard and heeded what Jesus taught. The foolish man heard but did not obey the teachings of Jesus. This is a sobering thought for us who read and hear God's Word. Many people are hearers, but how many obey what they hear? Later, James wrote, "Be doers of the word and not hearers only" (Jas. 1:22, HCSB).

Verses 28-29: **And it came to pass, when Jesus had ended these sayings, the people were astonished at his doctrine: [29]for he taught them as one having authority, and not as the scribes.**

The Sermon of the Mount was finished. Verses 28-29 record the crowd's initial response. Although Jesus was speaking primarily to His disciples, some of the crowd were listening; and they **were astonished at his doctrine** ("amazed at his teaching," NIV). The word translated **were astonished** literally means they "were struck out of themselves." What produced such a response? No doubt they were astonished at the content of Jesus' teachings, but Matthew quoted them as being impressed by His method of teaching. The people were accustomed to the teaching method of **the scribes.** The scribes quoted the famous teachers of the past and present as their authorities for what they said. But Jesus did not quote anyone or anything but the Scriptures—and He even claimed authority over them! Jesus spoke on His own **authority** (5:21-22,27-28,31-32,33-34,38-39,43-44).

What are some lasting truths in Matthew 7:24-29?

1. We should be eager, openhearted hearers of God's Word.
2. We need to put into practice what we hear.
3. Those who hear but do not heed the Word of God are not prepared for life's storms or for the final judgment.

❖ *Spiritual Transformations*

Jesus ended the Sermon on the Mount with an invitation to enter the narrow gate and follow the hard road. He warned against false prophets and said they could be recognized by their fruits. Jesus said that some will claim to have called on His name and done miracles in His name. But He said that the test of true discipleship was doing the Father's will. He emphasized the need to be doers of the Word and not hearers only.

Have you entered the door to salvation? ____ *Are you headed for heaven on the difficult road of committed discipleship?* ____

Why is it easier to hear Jesus' words than do them? ____________

*What will you do to become a fruitful doer rather than a fruitless hearer of Jesus' teaching?*____________________________________

____

Prayer of Commitment: Lord, my heart, my life, my all I give to You. Amen.

[1]Bruner, *The Christbook,* 283.
[2]Bruner, *The Christbook,* 286.